Proclaiming and Sustaining Excellence
Assessment as a Faculty Role

by Karen Maitland Schilling and Karl L. Schilling

ASHE-ERIC Higher Education Report Volume 26, Number 3

Prepared by

ERIC Clearinghouse on Higher Education
The George Washington University
URL: www.gwu.edu/~eriche

In cooperation with

Association for the Study
of Higher Education
URL: http://www.tiger.coe.missouri.edu/~ashe

Published by

Graduate School of Education and Human Development
The George Washington University
URL: www.gwu.edu

Jonathan D. Fife, Series Editor

Cite as

Schilling, Karen Maitland, and Karl L. Schilling. 1998. *Proclaiming and Sustaining Excellence: Assessment as a Faculty Role*. ASHE-ERIC Higher Education Report Volume 26, No. 3. Washington, D.C.: The George Washington University, Graduate School of Education and Human Development.

Library of Congress Catalog Card Number 98-85236
ISSN 0884-0040
ISBN 1-878380-83-4

Managing Editor: Lynne J. Scott
Manuscript Editor: Barbara Fishel/Editech
Cover Design by Michael David Brown, Inc., The Red Door Gallery, Rockport, ME

The ERIC Clearinghouse on Higher Education invites individuals to submit proposals for writing monographs for the *ASHE-ERIC Higher Education Report* series. Proposals must include:
1. A detailed manuscript proposal of not more than five pages.
2. A chapter-by-chapter outline.
3. A 75-word summary to be used by several review committees for the initial screening and rating of each proposal.
4. A vita and a writing sample.

ERIC Clearinghouse on Higher Education
Graduate School of Education and Human Development
The George Washington University
One Dupont Circle, Suite 630
Washington, DC 20036-1183

The mission of the ERIC system is to improve American education by increasing and facilitating the use of educational research and information on practice in the activities of learning, teaching, educational decision making, and research, wherever and whenever these activities take place.

This publication was prepared partially with funding from the Office of Educational Research and Improvement, U.S. Department of Education, under contract no. ED RR-93-002008. The opinions expressed in this report do not necessarily reflect the positions or policies of OERI or the Department.

EXECUTIVE SUMMARY

We are now over 10 years into the most recent wave of interest in assessment in higher education. In many states, publicly supported institutions of higher education have developed assessment programs in response to mandates from coordinating boards. All the regional accrediting associations articulate expectations for assessment, and attention to assessment has moved beyond publicly supported institutions into the private sector. National surveys of leaders in higher education suggest that assessment has been institutionalized quite broadly in American higher education.

These same surveys, however, suggest that campus leaders remain unconvinced about the real benefits of externally mandated assessment and fear misuse of its results. Moreover, although campuses nationwide (with a few notable exceptions) have responded to expectations for the development of assessment programs, faculty have not yet in any substantial numbers recognized and embraced local assessment efforts.

Proclaiming and Sustaining Excellence: Assessment as a Faculty Role explores the various sources of faculty's resistance to assessment and suggests ways to approach assessment that are more congenial to the traditional faculty role. In addressing administrators and faculty, the authors identify major conceptual, methodological, and policy advances over the past decade that may facilitate the faculty's greater engagement with assessment. Administrators are provided with useful frameworks for understanding the faculty's resistance and suggestions for approaches to assessment that respond to these sources of resistance. Faculty are provided with ways of thinking about assessment that comport more naturally with their traditional understandings of the faculty role in the academy.

What Advances in Assessment Make It More Congenial to Faculty?

Eight major shifts have occurred in the broad frameworks that have informed assessment practice: (1) focusing on the development of talent rather than simply displaying resources; (2) moving away from assuring minimal competency; (3) broadening the focus beyond linear, goal-centered approaches; (4) highlighting epistemological differences among the disciplines; (5) redirecting the focus to students and their learning processes; (6) making direct ties to teaching practice; (7) thinking of improvement as a continuing agenda; and (8) attending to the politics underlying judgments of effectiveness. Each of these broad theoretical shifts has shaped developing assessment practice to make it more congenial to faculty interests and dispositions.

Five broad changes in practice or assessment methods are also discussed: (1) fitting measures to a local context; (2) seeking convergence of multiple measures; (3) involving new disciplinary perspectives; (4) valuing authenticity; and (5) distinguishing between measurement and judgment.

Changing policies governing assessment include (1) changing notions of accountability; (2) the move to performance indicators; (3) barriers to the institutionalization of assessment; (4) false starts that incur hostility from the faculty; and (5) significant inroads on campuses toward the acceptance of assessment.

How Have Different Institutions Approached Assessment?

Practices at several institutions have been cited repeatedly in the literature on assessment over the past two decades. Specific institutional contexts and cultures have enabled or fostered the development of very different approaches to assessment at each institution. Six different institutional approaches are described: (1) assessment as part of an institution's fabric; (2) assessment as related to accountability; (3) assessment as an administrative service; (4) assessment as scholarship; (5) assessment as an opportunity for teaching; and (6) assessment as an add-on responsibility. Campuses where assessment falls into one of these categories are discussed in terms of the role faculty play in assessment.

How Can Assessment Be Viewed as a Faculty Role?

Six conditions are necessary if faculty are to view assessment as an integral part of their role:

1. Assessment must be embedded in a fiscal and policy context that supports innovation under administrative leadership providing vision and support.
2. Assessment must be grounded in significant questions that faculty find interesting.
3. Assessment must rely on evidence and forms of judgment that disciplinary specialists find credible.

4. Assessment must be rooted in a language and metaphors appropriate to the context.
5. Assessment must be identified as a stimulus to reflective practice.
6. Assessment must accommodate the nature of faculty life in the academy.

Proclaiming and Sustaining Excellence concludes by offering a set of principles for developing effective assessment programs that will engage faculty in meaningful assessment.

CONTENTS

It is natural that faculty have a healthy—even an unhealthy—suspicion of assessment or review of their teaching and students' learning. After all, throughout their lives, whether as K–12 students, undergraduate students, graduate students, or faculty seeking promotion and tenure, review of faculty performance has occurred for only two reasons: to accept them or to reject them. Why should the current trend for the assessment of faculty teaching and student learning be any different? Will the results not be the same? Will a faculty member not be reviewed favorably with something good to follow or reviewed unfavorably with something bad to follow?

Faculty members' aversion to assessment is also grounded in their personal experience with the process. Anyone who has been around higher education for any length of time has seen some form of assessment process produce dysfunctional results. There are several reasons for such outcomes. The most common is that there may be no strong link between why something is being assessed and the results. Without a clear connection between the purpose of assessment and the process of assessment, it is understandable how the outcomes may not achieve the desired impact. A second reason that assessment has failed is the use of inappropriate or incomplete methodology. For example, if the only tool used in the assessment of a course is evaluations by students, then a large part of assessing the course, such as the extent of coverage of the knowledge base or the level of students' competence, will be missing from the overall findings. Because of failures to establish a clear purpose and sound methodology for assessment, those using the assessment data are often confused about what the data mean and how they should interpret them. Finally, institutions often fear the negative impact of bad news. Consequently, when the results of assessment are negative, the data are often withheld and any information one could learn from the data is not available.

While the past fears and failures of assessment are understandable, there is no denying the increased pressure being placed on higher education to produce more evaluative data about its activities. Leading this pressure for more accountability are the expectations of stakeholders—students, parents, employers, and taxpayers. Although these stakeholders still hold higher education in high esteem, they want more concrete evidence that what is being promised is being delivered. One way to demonstrate the quality of an activity is to compare it with the results of other similar activities—with some past performance data of the same activity or with similar activities in other areas of the institution or at difference institutions. Moreover, as people's faith increases in computers' ability to analyze assessment data and as computers are more easily programmed to handle increasingly complex data, more reliance is placed on the results of assessment. Because people are increasingly coming to expect assessment data in all other areas of their lives, they no longer are content with the lack of assessment data related to higher education.

No matter what is driving the increased pressure for assessment, a fundamental truth is that the underlying assumptions that create an assessment process determine the results. The accuracy of the assumptions, the careful linking of these assumptions with the process, and the interpretation of the findings depend on who is involved in the assessment process. Consequently, faculty must get involved with the assessment of teaching and learning, or someone else will make the decisions about the basic assumptions that form the process of assessment.

This report, *Proclaiming and Sustaining Excellence: Assessment as a Faculty Role,* by Karen Maitland Schilling, professor of psychology, and Karl L. Schilling, scholar in residence in the office of residence life, both at Miami University (Ohio), examines the faculty's role in assessment. After carefully developing a context for assessment, the authors look at the conceptual, methodological, and policy advances made in the assessment of teaching and learning. They conclude with examples of the important role faculty can play in designing and implementing assessment at an institution.

With over 60 percent of the states considering or implementing performance-based funding and more capital campaigns raising funds that are categorically designated for specific outcomes, assessment of the teaching/learning process is no longer an option. Assessment is a fact of life. The faculty's involvement is a necessity if an acceptable balance is to be struck between the expectations of the spectator stakeholders and the faculty participants. The Schillings' report helps us to understand this partnership.

Jonathan D. Fife
Series Editor,
Professor of Higher Education Administration, and
Director, ERIC Clearinghouse on Higher Education

INTRODUCTION

This section begins and ends by laying out the premise for this book: Faculty have an important role to play in assessment. Following some discussion about definitions of assessment and a brief history of the assessment movement, it looks at the national context for the current assessment movement in higher education, exploring both the national and state political realities in which higher education works as well as the realities of faculty culture today in the context of a local campus. Speaking to both faculty and administrators, it identifies some of the major sources of faculty's resistance to engaging in meaningful assessment. The chapter ends by laying out the issues the rest of the monograph addresses.

A Definition of Assessment

"Assessment" has a range of meanings branching from its original etymological derivation "to sit beside." When the word "assessment" is used in this monograph, it refers to a range of methods for investigating the phenomenon and outcomes of students' learning. The usual purpose of assessment is to make judgments about the effects of instruction or curricula, with an aim toward improving them. This purpose is consistent with understandings advanced by recognized leaders in assessment today (e.g., Angelo 1995; Astin 1991; Marchese 1994). Important here are distinctions from potentially related, though differently focused, processes such as measurement, teaching evaluation, program evaluation, and grading of students.

The excess baggage associated with common use of the word "assessment," often including several of these related processes as opposed to the more narrow use suggested here, is a persistent source of confusion and some opposition to assessment on many campuses, particularly for faculty. For example, between their arrival as freshmen and their graduation at the end of the senior year, most students in American colleges and universities take 30 to 45 different courses (Pace 1979). They are tested 60 to 90 times or more, and 20 to 30 or more different faculty members make judgments about their performance. With all these evaluations, faculty ask, why would anyone call for assessment? The Statement on Assessment by the American Association of University Professors (1991) makes a similar observation, noting that American college students are the most tested in the world. Moreover, evaluations of courses and professors are used with considerable frequency on most American campuses today. Likewise, program review, which also is seen as a method for ensuring accountability and improving programs, has grown in popularity in American colleges and universities.

Though all of these processes involve data collection, the direct and intentional focus on improving teaching and learning is at the core of assessment. This focus is often missing in the grading of students or evaluation of programs or professors. Such a focus on improvement of learning often requires new efforts to collect data or the examination of existing data through a new lens. On most campuses, however, this distinction has not been made with sufficient clarity, resulting in a deserved cynicism about needing to provide more "useless data" and deep suspicion about intrusions into the proper province of the faculty, the curriculum and instruction, by other groups.

The Faculty's Role in Assessment

Much has been written about the need to know more about the impact of colleges and universities on students, most recently in broad-ranging discussions of standards (Adelman 1985, 1988; Stark and Thomas 1994). Similarly, a number of resources exist for those interested in techniques or strategies for assessing various programs (see, e.g., Erwin 1991; Gardiner, Anderson, and Cambridge 1997; Jacobi, Astin, and Ayala 1987; Nichols 1991). There is no shortage of materials on either why or how to do assessment. Although assessment programs exist on most campuses across the country and there is a lot of assessment going on, the impact of all this assessment on day-to-day functioning in the academy has been modest at best. Though we believe it is amenable to such transformation, assessment has not yet been adapted to the faculty culture within the academy. On many campuses, assessment happens in spite of rather than by or for the faculty. "If anything is to be accomplished in higher education, it is going to be done by the professors or it is not going to be done at all" (Rudolph 1984, p. 13). We share this understanding of change processes in higher education.

This monograph is about the role of faculty in assessment; thus, it invites a serious consideration of assessment as a faculty role. Despite ongoing national conversations about altering faculty roles and responsibilities (cf. Rice 1996), we do not here propose radical reformulations of the faculty role. Rather, we envision approaches to assessment that are congenial with traditional concepts of this role. We identify approaches to assessment that fit within historic definitions of the faculty's role.

Traditional concepts of the faculty role recognize three major components: teaching and advising, research and scholarship, and service. A first impulse in considering assessment as a faculty role is to align it with commitments for service. But, whether justified or not, service currently is the least valued of the components of the faculty role on most campuses. And it is the component of the faculty role that is least clearly defined and is least associated with historical traditions and precedents in the academy.

Rather, the expectations typically associated with teaching and advising and with research and scholarship should be clearly explicated and the expectations associated with assessment aligned with the widely understood expectations for those faculty roles. To satisfy common understandings of the faculty role in teaching and advising, professionals must stay current with subject matter in their field, convey an informed perspective, understand effective pedagogies, understand who their students are, evaluate student learning, give appropriate feedback, contribute to and oversee development of the curriculum, and participate in peer review. To satisfy common understandings of the faculty role in research and scholarship, professionals must contribute to the advancement of knowledge in their field, formulate interesting and relevant questions, pursue appropriate modes of inquiry, proceed with the investigation in systematic fashion, communicate results of findings, and respond appropriately to changes in their field. Expectations associated with effective assessment map neatly onto these two sets of expectations. Thus, the typical expectations of the role of assessment—seeking to improve students' learning, basing one's strategies in data about students and their performance, asking interesting questions, pursuing appropriate modes of inquiry, and using results and communicating them to appropriate constituencies—comport ideally with common understandings of the most important roles for faculty in the academy. Envisioning assessment in this way invites faculty involvement and control of the process.

As long as education has existed there have been questions about its effectiveness, the most compelling of which have been posed by educators themselves. Even if Plato and Socrates or Rousseau are not usually identified as progenitors of the modern assessment movement, the kinds of questions they posed about the effectiveness of educational strategies for achieving desired outcomes for students seem very similar to the questions directing current efforts at assessment. Do students have the right habits of mind? The focus of questioning in several of the *Dialogues* is mirrored in the ongoing discussions of the assessment of effectiveness of educational programs today. Socrates seemed never to provide a simple, straightforward answer to his students' questions but to issue more questions instead. Just as Socrates's questions unmasked the complexity of judging the effectiveness of various educational strategies, modern discussions of assessment need to evidence this same differentiation and complexity.

The Historical Backdrop
Historically, it is not only the great philosophers who have contributed to the rich history of thinking about the impact of educational programs on students, but also faculty and administrators, who in their daily work have created traditions and developed practices for gauging effectiveness. Indeed, the senior declamation and oral examination, the collective examination of the degree candidate by those who had instructed him, was common in American colleges until the end of the 19th century. That system declined in the face of the elective system and credit hour–driven degree requirements (Marchese 1987). At the beginning of this century, Abraham Flexner and President A. Lawrence Lowell of Harvard questioned how the competence of graduates could be assured with the demise of the senior declamation. With an identified core curriculum delivered to a relatively homogeneous student body of manageable size, the senior declamation functioned effectively as a mechanism of quality control. But with the growth of institutions, increasing variety of curricular offerings, and increasing diversity among students and their reasons for pursuing higher education, such uniform and obviously faculty-based approaches to assessment seemed less appropriate and less manageable as the strategy by which to judge the quality of education received.

Educational researchers also have laid strong foundations for understanding learning and learners, and have established a rich literature in measurement theory and practice to guide efforts to understand the effects of educational interventions. This development, particularly in the 1920s and 1930s, was a partial response to the demise of the senior declamation (Marchese 1987). Robert Pace, who spent a substantial portion of a long and distinguished career studying the outcomes of college, provides an overview of many of the most prominent large-scale studies in *Measuring Outcomes of College: Fifty Years of Findings and Recommendations for the Future* (1979). But often, faculty are "apprehensive about educational research and skeptical of its validity, [and] give the work such a low priority and status that their skepticism becomes self-fulfilling" (Bok 1986, p. 67). On few campuses have findings from educational researchers guided faculty decisions about the curriculum and instruction.

Developments in assessment theory and practice, some of which Pace chronicles, have continued rather steadily over time. In fact, at least six traditions of assessment inform the work between 1940 and the present: (1) assessment centers focused on assessment of human performance, common in the military, government, business, and industry; (2) assessment as learning, exemplified in Alverno College's curriculum based on explicit performance levels for identified abilities; (3) program monitoring involving large-scale longitudinal studies (such as Pace 1979); (4) studies of student development over the college years (in the tradition of Feldman and Newcomb 1969 or Pascarella and Terenzini 1991); (5) standardized testing; and (6) the "senior examiner," best exemplified in practice at Swarthmore (Marchese 1987).

Despite these rather focused traditions of assessment, broadly based calls for assessment in higher education have been far more episodic in character than persistent. As of 1987, American higher education had experienced two major assessment movements (Resnick and Goulden 1987). Each movement occurred after a period of major expansion accompanied by change in the undergraduate curriculum. The first occurred between 1918 and 1928, the second between 1952 and 1975. The turn to assessment after each of these periods of expansion has been associated with the goal of restoring substance and coherence to the undergraduate curriculum (Resnick and Goulden 1987). Importantly, each of these previous waves of interest in assessment had its origins in the legitimate concerns of faculty about the quality of the curriculum.

Each of these previous waves of interest in assessment had its origins in the legitimate concerns of faculty about the quality of the curriculum.

The Recent Wave of Interest in Assessment

Criticisms from within the academy

Calls for change, originating with insiders in the academy, provided early momentum for the most recent wave of interest in assessment. In the mid-1980s, two influential reports, written by and clearly intended for the higher education community, brought important focus to discussions. The first, *Involvement in Learning: Realizing the Potential of American Higher Education,* identified "three critical conditions for excellence in higher education," including student involvement, high expectations, and assessment and feedback (Study Group 1984).

> *Our colleges must value information far more than their current practices imply. They should make a conscientious effort to acquire and use better information about student learning, the effects of courses, and the impact of programs* (p. 21).

Integrity in the College Curriculum (Association 1985) sounded a similar strong call for assessment, terming it "scandalous" that we fail to assess the impacts of our teaching:

> *There must be ways of demonstrating to state legislatures, students, and the public at large that the colleges know what they are doing (or do not know) and that they are doing it well (or poorly). The colleges themselves must be held responsible for developing evaluations that the public can respect* (p. 33).

Harvard President Derek Bok added his voice to the chorus, calling for greater attention to assessment of the impact of the undergraduate educational experience:

> *No human endeavor can progress, except by chance, without some way of evaluating its performance. Only with assessment of this kind can faculties proceed by an intelligent process of trial and error to improve their educational programs* (Bok 1986, p. 66).

Interest in assessment in the academy relates to the historic privilege of the academy to be self-monitoring, to engage in quality control through peer review (Resnick and Goulden 1987). After the growth in enrollments and institutions' accommodating new students, often with the development of new curricula and new programs, a period of reflection and evaluation—a new wave of assessment—followed. One could speculate based on this history that, even absent external pressures, calls from within the academy might have been sufficient to generate another wave of increased interest in assessment. Most would argue, however, that it was the chorus of voices *outside* the academy that provided the strongest momentum behind the most recent wave of assessment in higher education.

Calls from outside the academy
In the 1970s and early 1980s, very serious questions were raised about the quality of elementary and secondary education in this country. The problems identified were numerous, complex, and multidimensional. Solutions proposed may not have related directly to a very thorough understanding of the problems being identified, but they were responses to loud calls for action. For example, broadly based standardized testing was proposed as a means of quality control. The National Governors Association quickly allied with this initiative, and soon testing for minimum competency became common practice in school systems across this country. If nothing else, this broad-scale testing at least represented a very visible response to the identification of problems with schools. And governors who were instrumental in implementing statewide testing for minimum competency in K–12 for the most part benefited in the public's eye from their association with the new talk of standards and testing to ensure quality.

It should come as no surprise, then, that when public attention increasingly focused on issues of quality and accountability in higher education, broad-scale assessment was advanced as an appropriate remedy for "the problem," though equally ill-defined. In 1986, the Education Commission of the States (ECS) issued a report, "Transforming the State Role in Improving Undergraduate Education," that identified eight challenges in undergraduate education, including improved assessment of students' and institutions' performance (Boyer et al. 1986). The report recommended monitoring the effectiveness of a state's system of higher education in meeting its

---

goals for undergraduate education, and encouraged each institution to develop its own "indicators of effectiveness" in undergraduate education. In responding to early initiatives for state accountability, however, the authors of the ECS report also offered some important and progressive cautions in articulating the importance of three principles to guide campus assessment: (1) distinguishing between assessment and testing; (2) using more than standardized tests of basic skills to measure the outcomes of undergraduate education; and (3) using assessment to improve teaching and learning.

Also in 1986, with states facing difficult fiscal situations and continued growth in the demands for support for public higher education, the National Governors Association issued yet another influential report. This one, clearly intended for an audience extending well beyond the higher education community and unabashedly titled *Time for Results,* brought a new focus to discussions of accountability in the academy.

> *Each college and university [should] implement systematic programs that use multiple measures to assess undergraduate student learning. The information gained from assessment should be used to evaluate institutional and program quality* (National Governors 1986, p. 161).

Not surprisingly, some initial rushes into the assessment fray in response to the governors' calls seemed to propose little more than "grown-up" versions of the standardized tests adopted in elementary and secondary schools; for example, in South Dakota, the Board of Regents mandated testing with the ACT-COMP at the end of the sophomore year and major field assessments using nationally normed instruments. This example is not meant to disparage the quality or utility of either college-level assessment or the parallel approaches used in the K–12 system, but to identify one source of resistance to assessment among college faculty. Drawing parallels between the work of the college professor and that of the elementary or high school teacher by suggesting similar approaches to assessment of student outcomes evokes considerable resentment and hostility from many college faculty.

Peter Ewell from the National Center for Higher Education Management Systems, one of the most influential voices on policy issues in assessment, describes the more common reaction to new assessment mandates for higher education:

In Washington, . . . an initial proposal for sophomore testing was turned into a study resolution. After a year of trying out four available general education examinations, it was concluded that not one of [them] was adequate for informing local improvement. In the three years that followed, most states came to the same conclusion, though few went to the same trouble to test alternatives. Through a combination of pure political opposition on the part of higher education leaders and sound reasoning about what might really cause campus-level change, most states adopted a different approach (Ewell 1993b, p. 343).

This "different approach" might be described more adequately as "different approaches." Initial concepts of centralized, statewide strategies to monitor quality and assure accountability gave way to a wide variety of highly decentralized approaches to quality improvement. Virginia offered one of the most progressive models of this sort. It did not include external monitoring within a broad comparative framework; instead, campuses responded to calls for greater attention to assessment, but their approaches were much more localized and tied to specific programmatic goals.

From his position as a policy analyst, Ewell expressed some regret about this movement toward decentralization and the variety of approaches to assessment. In his view, integrating disparate strategies would be required to meet the demands of accountability, for dissatisfaction with decentralized approaches to achieving credible accountability statewide would likely lead to continued interest in common outcomes testing among state leaders. Indeed, "the primary impact of assessment on state policy development has been to open new avenues for systematically considering academic issues traditionally considered off-limits to outside authorities" (Ewell 1993b, p. 352).

Before about 1985, consistent with a notion of accountability that emphasized access and efficiency, state authorities were concerned primarily with fiscal and administrative matters. Relevant academic policy issues were limited and typically included areas like admissions policy, student financial assistance, and program duplication. With the evolution of a new accountability for higher education based on statewide return on investment, assessment policies pioneered the notion that state government had a legitimate interest in what was taught and how. . . . In the nineties, state policy actions in the academic arena are becoming more comprehensive, proactive, and frequent, and in many ways, the actions are being shaped by the previous experience with assessment (Ewell 1993b, p. 349).

Although administrators on some campuses may be facing up to this new view of accountability, clearly the idea that state government has a legitimate interest in what is taught, how it is delivered, and by whom has not permeated the faculty culture on most campuses. Faculty strongly resist intrusions into what they see as their proper province, and they view curriculum and instruction as off-limits to outsiders. On many campuses, faculty have been motivated to take a proactive interest in assessment simply out of self-defense: "If we don't do it, then *they* will do it to us." This context is the one in which many of the local, campus-based approaches to assessment noted earlier were developed.

Unfortunately, assessment strategies developed to satisfy external demands for accountability and to ward off unwanted intrusions from outsiders may differ substantially from those that would be developed in a less highly charged context of thoughtful self-examination in the interest of improvement. Clearly, as Ewell has suggested, state mandates may be credited with providing a major impetus to the development of assessment practices in higher education nationally over the last decade. But it is much more difficult to document the desired program improvements resulting from state-mandated assessment. Tennessee and Missouri may provide such examples, but extending this list much beyond these two states is difficult.

The role of accrediting associations
From this perspective of program improvement, other external mandates for assessment—those from accrediting bodies—not only exerted additional pressures on institutions to engage in assessment, but also, particularly in their later iterations, placed a higher premium on campuses' uses of assessment data to improve teaching and learning. In 1988, under the leadership of Secretary William Bennett, the U.S.

Department of Education began to insist that both regional and programmatic accrediting bodies require information on students' achievement from institutions and programs as part of the accreditation process. In summary, the requirements of all six regional accrediting groups are to:

> . . . *develop and articulate clear goals stated in terms of outcomes, select or build appropriate local measures to gather evidence of goal achievement, and provide evidence of the ways that the resulting evidence was used to inform improvement* (Ewell 1993b, p. 345).

Several regional accrediting groups have chosen to focus on student outcomes and related attempts to improve teaching and learning as the expected loci for assessment. The Western Association of Schools and Colleges (WASC) has begun to consider alternatives to traditional self-study based on systematic consideration of institutional portfolios of data on effectiveness.

The process of peer review underlying both regional and specialized accreditation in this country has ensured that these new mandates for assessment have been negotiated rather than simply imposed. Conversations between representatives of accrediting groups and those from colleges and universities necessarily have acknowledged both the compelling external pressures for greater accountability in higher education and the long-standing traditions of institutional autonomy in colleges and universities. Because the self-study that forms the basis for accreditation typically involves faculty as well as administrative staff, and because accrediting groups have sought evidence that assessment has truly been institutionalized, it is likely that faculty's greater involvement in assessment has come as a result of mandates from accrediting groups rather than as a result of mandates from state controlling boards.

Moreover, because the reach of accrediting bodies extends beyond publicly supported institutions, mandates for assessment from these groups have extended not just to the public sector of American higher education, but also to private institutions.

National proactive movers
The evolution of national conversations about assessment in higher education has been shaped substantially by the actions

of professional associations and funding agencies. The Assessment Forum of the American Association for Higher Education (AAHE) brought focus to key issues, seeded some of the most important changes in thinking over time, and nurtured advances in thinking about assessment on campuses across the country by identifying themes for annual meetings, highlighting key questions, selecting keynote speakers and other conferences presenters, and providing opportunities for professional development through conference workshops. The forum assembled national leaders in assessment to produce an influential document, "Principles of Good Practice for Assessing Student Learning" (AAHE 1992); other papers published by the forum have either chronicled or foreshadowed many of the most important changes in the practice of assessment over time.

The work of Trudy Banta, vice chancellor for planning and institutional improvement at Indiana University–Purdue University Indianapolis, in establishing and continuing to edit *Assessment Update,* a newsletter that has appeared six times yearly since 1989, and sharing institutional stories about assessment as well as articles on policy, practice, and methods, significantly amplified the impact of AAHE's Assessment Forum and contributed to a broadened understanding of assessment. Through this publication, other edited volumes (Banta and Associates 1993; Banta, Lund, Black, and Oblander 1996), various other writings (Banta 1985a, 1985b, 1986, 1988, 1989, 1992, 1995, 1996; Borden and Banta 1994), an annual national workshop-based assessment conference, and an annual international conference on assessment and quality assurance, Banta has made some of the most significant contributions to bringing both exposure and coherence to a broad array of assessment activities on campuses across the country.

In a number of states, most notably South Carolina, Virginia, and Colorado, assessment coordinating networks were established to help institutions respond to state initiatives for assessment. These networks were designed to bring together faculty and administrators from throughout the state to share experiences with assessment, to bring national leaders in assessment to speak at annual conferences, and to provide a support network for facilitating institutional learning about current best practices in assessment. Reid Johnson, a faculty member at Winthrop University, provided the initial leadership to help establish the national prominence of the South Carolina network in these efforts. The networks facilitated the participation of faculty members in discussions of assessment without the expense of travel to national conferences, provided opportunities for professional development for faculty, and facilitated collaboration on a shared problem—how to respond most effectively to state mandates—among institutions that traditionally may have been rivals. The networks helped establish assessment as the responsibility of faculty and provided resources to help faculty identify the potential benefits of assessment for their daily work.

Because expectations for assessment arrived on the scene at a time of contracting resources in higher education, the role of external funding in supporting exploration of new approaches to assessment was critical. In its beginning years, the AAHE Assessment Forum was supported by a grant from the Department of Education's Fund for the Improvement of Post-Secondary Education (FIPSE). For a number of years, assessment was a priority area for FIPSE grant funding, and FIPSE supported many national leaders in assessment in their efforts. Models of best practices were encouraged and broadly disseminated with the assistance of FIPSE. The series *Lessons Learned from FIPSE Projects* (Marcus 1990; Marcus, Cobb, and Shoenberg 1993, 1996) highlights a number of the most influential of these projects, ranging from Alverno College's very successful emphasis on assessment as learning, to Tennessee's and Missouri's models of incentive funding, to general education assessment at the University of Connecticut and Miami University. Exxon, Ford, Kellogg, and other foundations have supported other important assessment initiatives.

Based on a survey of members of the National Association of State Universities and Land-Grant Colleges (NASULGC), some of the best known assessment programs are at small colleges and less selective universities.

Based on a survey of members of the National Association of State Universities and Land-Grant Colleges (NASULGC), some of the best known assessment programs are at small colleges and less selective universities.

It is those who felt that they were doing an excellent job with the kinds of students entering their institutions, but who were not getting proper recognition [because of] the research-oriented status system of American postsecondary education, who led the outcomes assessment movement in the U.S. It is the "Rodney Dangerfields" seeking respect, not those who already had that

respect through research and graduate instruction,
who have embraced outcomes assessment as a means to
show their own excellence. Small wonder, then, that
major research universities have been slow to jump on
the bandwagon, particularly since the benefits of doing
so have not always been obvious (Muffo 1991, p. 12).

Although some criticize the absence of other models of
higher education beyond that offered by selective, research-
oriented universities (see, e.g., Jencks and Riesman 1968),
the assessment movement has had one very positive result:

In retrospect, it appears that the outcomes assessment
movement has finally added another respected model,
one based on showing student intellectual, social, and
ethical growth. It is now more acceptable in academe,
and is highly regarded among the general public, to be a
nonselective institution [that] produces substantial growth
among undergraduate students of differing backgrounds.
The excellent undergraduate institution, measured in
student learning as opposed to incoming selectivity, pro-
vides a much needed alternative to the model described
by Jencks and Riesman (Muffo 1991, pp. 12–13).

Most institutions of higher education in this country are not
selective, research-oriented universities. Faculty can be excited about the prospects of substantiating the excellence of
the programs offered by their institutions to students under
this new broadened understanding of what it means to be
an excellent college or university.

Why calls for accountability now? Will they go away?
One might reasonably ask whether the concerns about quality
in higher education are so serious as to provoke such a widespread response as these broadly based assessment mandates.
Though comparisons of test scores of elementary and secondary students in this country to those of students in other
countries might suggest problems with these schools, no similar comparative disadvantage is noted for higher education.
Indeed, students from all over the world are still drawn to
institutions of higher education in the United States in higher
numbers than they are to anywhere else. Moreover, economic
analyses suggest that pursuing higher education clearly pays

off. Lifetime earnings for college graduates dramatically outpace those of individuals who complete only high school. Yet calls for the accountability of higher education, beginning in earnest in the late 1970s or early 1980s, persist.

The nature of these demands has changed over time, however. Criticism currently seems less focused and intense than was the case a decade earlier, but all indicators suggest that higher education will enter the new millennium under continuing scrutiny. And policy makers now seem much more inclined to direct their criticisms to the heart of the academic enterprise—what ought to be taught and how it ought to be taught—than was previously the case. The heyday of largely unquestioning acceptance and respect for institutions of higher education is long past.

The public is more cynical about all kinds of institutions, and colleges and universities will not escape questioning about their functioning. Much of the cynicism has been aimed directly at faculty and their workload. As other institutions were forced to downsize, the life of the faculty member in academe was seen as overprivileged and unrealistic. Indeed, even Garry Trudeau took on a number of issues related to faculty workload and lack of attention to students and quality teaching in *Doonesbury*. This cynicism may well affect the accustomed missions of many institutions as the public calls for greater emphasis on the development of workers' skills and their employability as indicators of colleges' and universities' effectiveness.

College costs have escalated at the same time we have witnessed the end of the pattern of graduates' financial leapfrogging over the previous generation, and college graduates today can no longer expect to exceed their parents' income. Demands for access to higher education have introduced additional challenges to traditional concepts of effectiveness. More diverse student populations with more diverse needs and goals strain our previous understandings of institutions' effectiveness.

Growth of participation nationally
Before 1982, about one-third of the states required that institutions conduct regular program reviews, but almost none required explicit reporting on outcomes (Ewell 1993b). By 1993, all but nine states had an assessment policy in place governing public institutions of higher education. The survey

of campus trends reported in 1992 that 92 percent of the nation's colleges and universities engaged in some form of assessment (El-Khawas 1992). And virtually all campuses today would claim to be involved in some form of assessment.

Beginning in the late 1970s and early 1980s, observers have commented consistently about the faculty's fear of and resistance to assessment. Ironically, the very faculty and institutions that asserted the inability to measure the impacts of their programs were themselves involved in developing evaluation methods for virtually every other kind of organization in the culture (Adamany 1979). Faculty seemed quite willing to turn their critical lenses and analytical frameworks on the work of everyone but themselves. What factors might account for the faculty's resistance to looking at their own enterprise?

Until recently, the higher education community saw little point but no small threat in the explicit assessment of student outcomes. The positive impact of college upon the student remains an almost righteously unexamined premise—the "great self-evident" of higher education (Ewell 1983, p. 1).

"Until recently" suggests a sea change among faculty beginning in the early 1980s. Despite administrative action to respond to calls for assessment, however, it is not at all clear that the transition has occurred among faculty on many campuses. Many faculty continue to assert that those things most valuable in undergraduate education would indeed be the most difficult to measure—values rather than skills, dispositions or attitudes toward learning and knowledge rather than collections of facts.

Faculty are reluctant to become involved in assessment for three main reasons: (1) fear that information about outcomes, if collected and widely disseminated, would reflect badly on those collecting it; (2) the belief that many, if not most, important outcomes of higher education are qualitative and cannot therefore be objectively measured; and (3) apprehension about the "false precision" inherent in quantified outcome criteria (Ewell 1983). These same factors, and perhaps some new ones, contribute to the faculty's reluctance to become involved in assessment to the present day. The survey of NASULGC members mentioned earlier echoes Ewell's list in identifying several problems with assessment: costs, pressures on funding, the misuse of data, and the faculty's skepticism, fears, and resistance (Muffo 1991). Similarly, the results of an ACT survey of two- and four-year public colleges about assessment in higher education notes that "despite exemplary efforts in outcomes assessment, results for the majority of assessment programs have been disappointing" (Steele 1996, p. 12). Over 50 percent of the survey's respondents identified getting faculty to be involved and devote time to assessment as a significant problem.

> *Faculty are simply going to resist assessment and accountability. It's uncomfortable to be judged, especially on the achievement of others, such as one's students. The process of assessment is time-consuming and can be frustrating; there are no easy answers. Faculty cannot completely control the process and results* (Muffo 1996, p. 1).

Sources of Faculty Resistance

Resistance can be viewed simply as opposition. The privileged faculty do not want to recognize changing realities; they are set in their ways and unable to respond to the need for changes in the academy. Such a view engenders only frustration and negativism, providing little focus and hope for change. But the faculty's resistance can also be viewed as a positive force: a defense of central components of life in the academy associated with traditional definitions of the faculty's role that have served higher education well for centuries. From this latter perspective, understanding resistance becomes an important task in any strategy for changing an organization.

Workshops at national meetings and on campuses across the country over the past five years have explored the issue of resistance with faculty. The sources of their resistance to assessment appear to be very similar across campuses and can be reduced to a dozen concerns that should be addressed in the implementation of any campus assessment policy.

1. *We already do it.* One of faculty's first responses to assessment on virtually every campus is to identify the number of evaluative processes in which they are already involved. Faculty report that they grade students day in and day out, and most faculty report that grading is one

of the things about teaching they like least. Faculty also argue that they evaluate their classes and instruction regularly and therefore see assessment as redundant. Few campuses do not include evaluations of courses and professors as part of their regular reviews. And the thought of doing more evaluation is deadening. Faculty generally do not understand what more is being asked of them by those calling for assessment. Yet few assessment policies provide a straightforward statement of the difference between other evaluative processes and assessment.

2. *The data will be misused.* Campus assessment policies do not appear out of the blue in the lives of faculty, and no campus starts fresh with a blank slate. Rather, new policies operate in contexts that have been shaped by long institutional histories. Faculty members' apprehension about the unknown feeds on negative experiences with the institution in the past, for virtually every campus has a story about data collected avowedly for one purpose that are used for a totally different purpose. Faculty fear that data on assessment will be used against them in some way they cannot anticipate. Data collected to identify potential areas for improving programs may suddenly become the focus of discussions for reviewing or eliminating programs. Or data collected to examine a program's effectiveness may become the focus during reviews for promotion, tenure, and salary increases. Moreover, faculty have plenty of experience with completing surveys and other forms of gathering data that lead nowhere. Thus, rivaling faculty's fear that data will be used against them is the fear that painstakingly collected assessment data will not be used at all—that the lengthy survey that took considerable time to complete will simply be filed away and forgotten.

3. *I'm afraid of change.* Whether assessment is about improvement or accountability, the implicit message is that change is needed. Many faculty feel that they are already working very hard and doing a good job, and they do not welcome the message that change is needed. Faculty fear the slippery slope represented by assessment. Moving away from familiar turf, they ask with some anxiety, "What will they have me do next?"

4. *The criteria are unclear.* It is not at all clear to many faculty how assessment data once collected will be evalu-

Faculty view many of the attempts to assess the effectiveness of academic programs as hopelessly reductionist.

ated. They do not know the set of standards against which performance will be measured, and they do not know that they can trust how the data will be interpreted. Faculty believe that they cannot afford to demonstrate that they are not doing a good job, yet they often feel that they do not know the basis upon which assessment data are to be evaluated. Because most teaching takes place behind closed doors and because most faculty have not been trained in pedagogy or the development of curriculum, many faculty (who have a natural proclivity to be highly self-critical) fear that they may be doing a "bad" job and that assessment will "find them out."

5. *Assessment violates my academic freedom.* Faculty are generally suspicious of any initiative that potentially invades sacred turf: their freedom in the classroom to discuss what they teach. The specter of "teaching to the test" overshadowed many of the earliest discussions of state-mandated assessment. "While it is true that, thus far, the assessment movement does not appear to have resulted in any overt infringement of academic freedom as traditionally understood, the question remains whether, in more subtle ways, assessment may begin to shape the planning and conduct of courses" (American Association 1991, p. 51). Faculty tend to resist any threat to their right to choose how and what to teach.

6. *Assessment is inconsistent with academic values.* Faculty view many of the attempts to assess the effectiveness of academic programs as hopelessly reductionist. They believe that the complexity of their work with students often is not appreciated or appropriately represented in many approaches to the assessment of student outcomes. They resist the logic behind the desire to engage in the kinds of comparative judgments among institutions that drive many state-mandated assessment programs, viewing such movement as a threat to the multiplicity and diversity of institutions and programs. The report of the AAUP's Committee C questions whether mandated assessment "tends to diminish the autonomy and discourage the uniqueness of individual campuses" (American Association 1991, p. 51), arguing that "even a reasoned recognition of institutional differences of the sort that mandated assessment plans claim to recognize may result in the stifling of growth and development in an insti-

They believe that the complexity of their work with students often is not appreciated or appropriately represented in many approaches to the assessment of student outcomes.

tution in the process of change, or the favoring of one campus with a particular set of goals over another in the same system" (p. 52). The AAUP resists what it would identify as the move toward homogenization and erasure of the differences in institutional exemplars of "good practice" in assessment, reasoning that it is necessary "to consider whether a model devised at one type of institution . . . is necessarily—or properly—transferable to other kinds of institutions" (p. 52). Ideally within the academy, respect is accorded to expertise. Many faculty question what they perceive to be the deprofessionalization of the faculty associated with many approaches to assessment. Faculty ask why they got a Ph.D. in French literature to try to function as a second-class statistician. Of all methods of assessment, faculty seem to prefer evaluation by respected peers to any other method (Banta 1995). Faculty can be expected to respond more favorably to approaches that value expertise and professionalism and appropriately represent complexity.

7. *Faculty lack knowledge of assessment.* Many faculty resist assessment because they simply do not understand what it entails and how they would go about doing it. They have no professional background that prepares them to examine questions related to the effectiveness of current teaching strategies for facilitating learning. Many have observed that typical faculty have come to higher education with little preparation in teaching. Outside of faculty in education and social science disciplines, the typical faculty member has little to no exposure to a knowledge base in assessment. Every campus likely has a small group of faculty who focus some of their energies on discussions outside their disciplines, on issues of concern in the larger higher education community. Among such groups, discussions of assessment may sound familiar chords. For the vast majority of faculty on most campuses, however, assessment is not a topic with which they have even passing familiarity.

8. *I have no confidence in existing instruments.* Although a lack of knowledge of assessment would lead many faculty to defer to the judgment of those more knowledgeable in this area, these same faculty are able to identify the limits of available methodologies for indexing the effectiveness of their daily work with students. They are quite capable of identifying the gaps between what they

teach and what is measured by available methods, and they have little confidence in the results generated by those methods, finding them of little value in improving their teaching.

9. *Too often, what is tested becomes what is valued.* Faculty, recognizing the gaps between their aspirations for what higher education can provide for students and what tests can easily measure, fear that what can be easily assessed will be what is valued. Many faculty, particularly those in liberal arts disciplines, spend a good deal of their time with students focused on developing dispositions and values, yet skills and performances are more easily measured than dispositions and values. Mastery of content is more easily assessed than thinking processes, and immediate impacts are certainly more easily measured than long-term effects.

10. *We don't need more bureaucracy.* Faculty on many campuses believe that they could improve students' learning more effectively and more efficiently by using resources dedicated to assessment for other purposes. They are not persuaded that assessment and students' learning are linked. And they do not believe that the results of assessment justify the costs. They can, however, identify new layers of bureaucracy devoted to satisfying mandates for accountability that are supported by dollars that could instead directly support instruction.

11. *My plate is too full.* Faculty members' perceived resistance to assessment in many instances may not be rooted in opposition or hostility to anything about assessment itself. It could simply be rooted in faculty members' feeling that they are already overburdened. Many faculty find the thought of taking on yet another agenda item overwhelming. As resources have either contracted or not expanded and demands on faculty time have grown, many faculty believe that they already have too much on their plates and that even if assessment were a "good thing," they cannot take on another one. "More cannot be added to each faculty member's 'To Do List'; either some responsibilities will have to be set aside temporarily, or assessment will have to be meaningfully integrated into ongoing activities" (Ferren 1993, p. 3).

12. *Nobody told me about the shift from teachers and teaching to students and learning.* Assessment calls for a focus

on the learning outcomes of students. Professional associations in higher education have devoted a great deal of
attention to the need to shift from a focus on teachers
and teaching to a focus on students and learning. Many
faculty have not been part of these conversations, however, and either do not fully understand the implications
of this shift for their day-to-day conduct or simply reject
some of the underlying premises of the arguments for
the importance of this changed perspective. Without
agreement about this "prior issue," conversations about
assessment are very difficult to move forward.

Historically, faculty have been committed to the development of excellence in the programs they are part of. Indeed,
an important role for faculty has been to contribute to activities that earn recognition for both the individual and the program. Professional pride for faculty has been based on assert-
ing quality in some area, whether in teaching, students' performance, research, publishing, procuring grant support, or
service. Many of these assertions of quality, however, have
been based not on objective data, but on campus traditions,
personal beliefs, or anecdotes.

Many faculty continue to focus their time and energies on
improving the experience of students, and some are aided in
this endeavor by systematic data collection. Some faculty
may have been persuaded of the importance of doing a better job of telling their own stories about institutional effectiveness to various constituencies outside higher education,
and have been aided in this process by assessment data. Faculty will continue to be committed to proclaiming and sustaining the excellence of their programs. They can be expected, however, to resist a focus on students as customers
and education as a product to be sold. And faculty will continue to resist involvement in assessment when they perceive
that the terms are set by those outside the academy.

The following sections identify conceptual, methodological, and policy advances in assessment over time. The categories overlap to some extent; for example, most conceptual
or theoretical advances involve methodological change, and
methods influence political and policy considerations. But
despite its obvious limitations, this framework seems useful
for outlining important developments in assessment. The
intention is for a reader who reviews this outline of the his-

tory of assessment in higher education to benefit from the wisdom of steps taken by others without having to retrace the actual steps themselves in designing or considering their own approach to assessment.

CONCEPTUAL OR THEORETICAL ADVANCES

This section identifies eight major shifts in the broad frameworks that have informed assessment practice over the past decade: (1) focusing on the development of talent rather than simply displaying resources; (2) moving away from assuring minimal competency; (3) broadening the focus beyond linear, goal-centered approaches; (4) highlighting epistemological differences among the disciplines; (5) redirecting the focus to students and their learning processes; (6) making direct ties to teaching practice; (7) thinking of improvement as a continuing agenda; and (8) attending to the politics underlying judgments of effectiveness. We suggest ways in which each broad theoretical shift has shaped developing assessment practice to make it more congenial to faculty's interests and dispositions. Each innovation identified grew out of a broad critique of common assessment practices. And each innovator has, directly or indirectly, offered suggestions for the design of approaches to assessment that might be better suited for contemporary higher education. A common theme in all of these arguments is that many initial approaches to assessment in higher education have been simplistic and reductionist, providing little information that will be of value, particularly to faculty, in improving students' educational experiences.

The Talent Development or Value-Added Perspective

Our assessment efforts are handicapped in part because we are not really very clear about what we are trying to accomplish, and in part because we perpetuate questionable practices out of sheer habit, for convenience, or to fulfill purposes that are unrelated or at best tangential to the basic mission of our colleges and universities (Astin 1991, p. 20).

What are we trying to accomplish in our institutions of higher education? What is our mission? Astin suggested that we should be about developing talent or "adding value," and contrasted this approach to understanding effectiveness to the traditional "resource" or "reputational" views. If one focuses on resource or reputation, entering students are under the lens. Excellence in this framework relates to enrolling the most impressive student body—with the highest possible grades or test scores. Excellent institutions from this perspective are those with bright students, not necessarily those that educate them well. Assessment then amounts to counting the riches, which may be as diverse as the number of books in the library, the size of the endowment, or faculty members' degrees. Excellence is defined by the quality of the collection and gives rise to an inherent narcissism or egocentrism (Astin 1991). Under this model, excellence can rightly be attributed more to the quality of performance of the admissions and financial aid office staffs than to the quality of the faculty's efforts in carrying out their responsibilities.

The important question here is whether graduates' achievements exceed the levels that would have been predicted simply by extrapolating information from their abilities at entry.

Many approaches to assessment that focus on the achievements of advanced students or graduates also fall within this reputational or resource perspective. The logic here is quite simple: If an institution's graduates are excellent, certainly the institution itself must be excellent. Testing bright students at the time of completion of their academic programs will usually yield impressive bragging rights. And, in fact, many of this country's elite institutions make expansive claims about the impact of their programs based upon graduates' accomplishments. But these same students were bright when they entered college. It is not surprising, then, that they are still bright when they graduate. The important, and most often unasked, question here is whether graduates' achievements exceed the levels that would have been predicted simply by extrapolating information from their abilities at entry. Are they doing better than they would have done had they been left alone? Many institutional assessment programs may not even demonstrate that their educational programs do no harm to students.

Further, using resource or reputational models of excellence as a framework for assessment beyond this country's elite institutions offers minimal promise. Ensuring access to a broad range of students is a central component of the mission of many institutions in this country's very diverse system of higher education, and evaluating quality based on entry-level abilities would be absolutely inconsistent with this mission. According to Astin, education is fundamentally concerned with change and growth and development in students. Resource or reputational concepts of excellence miss this important point. From the perspective of talent development or value added, attention is directed to changes or growth in students over time. Talent developed or value added relates to the quality or quantity of learning and development. Excellence, from this perspective, is a function of how well we educate our students.

*The basic premise underlying the talent development
concept is that true excellence lies in the institution's ability to affect its students and faculty favorably, to enhance
their intellectual and scholarly development, to make a
positive difference in their lives* (Astin 1991, p. 25).

The focus on enhancing learning and development in the
talent development model relates without difficulty to what
most faculty see as their role and responsibilities in the academy. Although faculty may be interested in teaching good
students, it is not the case that most faculty would enthusiastically invest their time and energies in assessment related to
resource and reputational concepts of excellence. Faculty
are, however, concerned about whether what they do with
students makes a difference—the focus of a talent development model of assessment.

The Failure of Minimum Competency Testing
One would not first look to the president of this country's
largest testing company for cautions about assessment, for
one would expect that person to strongly advocate testing.
Nevertheless, Gregory Anrig, former president of Educational Testing Service and a former commissioner of education for the commonwealth of Massachusetts, offers some of
the most persuasive arguments against the use of "minimum
competency" to ensure accountability in higher education.
Based on a report by the U.S. General Accounting Office:

> . . . *estimates of the number of standardized tests ad-
> ministered annually in the public schools range from
> 30 [million] to 127 million, and their costs are estimated
> to be anywhere from $100 million to $910 million per
> year (if you include indirect costs). [But] with the ex-
> ception of some improvement in achievement [of] basic
> skills . . . , this investment in accountability testing has
> done little to change the rather dismal learning results
> that continue to be the nationwide focus of school re-
> form. . . . There is a rather naive belief abroad in the
> land that all you need to do to get better educational
> outcomes is to give a test and publish the results. If this
> were true, we wouldn't have the problems we do with
> inadequate student achievement levels. . . . The key to
> successful assessment is that information on educa-*

tional outcomes actually gets used to improve educational opportunity (Anrig 1993, pp. 2–3).

Much of the testing based on minimal competency has served as a report card on systems or schools or programs rather than as a diagnostic aid that might suggest appropriate interventions to improve outcomes.

Anrig had earlier offered a less dismal summary judgment of minimal competency testing for the elementary and secondary grades, but he had urged governors and state legislators to avoid this approach to ensuring accountability for higher education. Issuing strong cautions to lawmakers against shortcuts and expediency that might result in little improvement and lots of standardization, he warned, "Shortcuts to stronger standards in colleges and universities can reduce diversity and promote conformity in higher education" (Anrig 1986, p. 6). Minimal competency testing simply would not work for higher education, he said, and identified four reasons why externally imposed standards for minimal competency would be a mistake:

1. Historically, the responsibility for setting instructional policies and standards rested with the institution and, more specifically, with the faculty. "If efforts to improve student performance are to work, the institutions must be stimulated to act. Government cannot do it for them" (p. 2).
2. Equating higher education with the attainment of minimal competency is to "contradict and undermine its very purpose" (p. 2). Clearly, no institution of higher education aspires to ensure minimal competency, as colleges and universities operate on the assumption that students are minimally competent before they enroll. They aspire to something "higher."
3. Complex and diverse systems of higher education quite appropriately would have a great deal of difficulty gaining consensus on what is essential. Institutions of higher education have very different functions, they identify very different missions for themselves, and they share no consensus on what they are about. Yet such agreement on "essential" is a necessary precondition for any generally applied assessment program.
4. Tests alone cannot evaluate institutions of higher education, any more than they can evaluate other complex

entities. Complex judgments requiring multiple sources of data are required to make such evaluations.

Certain approaches to assessment would lead to the improvement of higher education: (1) focusing on higher levels of mastery rather than minimal standards; (2) asking faculty to determine appropriate learning outcomes for students at their institutions; (3) ensuring that the process and results relate directly to institutional improvement; (4) ensuring that faculty and students feel that the results of assessment are useful to them and help them improve performance; and (5) moving beyond a test to think broadly about the range of available and relevant data discovered (Anrig 1986).

Few faculty see minimal competency testing as even vaguely related to the work they do, at best identifying it as a way to quickly dispose of unwanted responsibilities for assessment. And it is difficult to identify examples of the productive use of minimal competency testing to improve curricula and instruction at our nation's colleges and universities.

Beyond Linear, Goal-Centered Approaches

Must assessment start with goals? Perhaps because of his extensive experience with accreditation of colleges and universities, Ralph Wolff, executive director of the Western Association of Schools and Colleges, recognized the gap between textbook models of organizational functioning—the "rational choice model"—and day-to-day experience in the academy. While setting goals may be strongly advocated as the appropriate starting point for assessment, Wolff (and many others) recognized that it is hardly the operative mode in most institutions of higher education. Some might argue that the absence of clearly specified, agreed-upon goals is a major problem in higher education today. According to Wolff, the more complex our institutions, the more variegated our institutional mission statements, and the more diverse our philosophical and epistemological perspectives, the less useful and appropriate may be the processes that aim toward collective goal setting. Within such a complex framework, institutional goals may need to be stated at such a global and generic level as to be minimally useful in guiding assessment.

As useful as the goal-oriented model of assessment may be, . . . it is just one way to approach assessment; in

*many ways it is not the best way, and it certainly should
not be prescribed as the only way. Such an approach is
essentially hierarchical, linear, deductive: It first estab-
lishes a broad principle—a goal—and then moves toward stating the goal in sufficiently specific terms to
assess its accomplishment* (Wolff and Astin 1990, p. 10).

Institutions differ in some important ways with regard to the
ease of setting goals:

*In some institutions, particularly relatively small and ho-
mogeneous ones such as liberal arts or church-affiliated
colleges, it may be possible to achieve consensus on goals
with a reasonable expenditure of time and effort, in
which case organizing assessment activities around goals
may be entirely appropriate. But for many institutions,
particularly larger, more complex ones, focusing energy
on goal specification can be . . . enormously labor-
intensive and unproductive. . . . If work gets bogged down
at the outset in this way, the entire assessment effort may
be at risk. Or the goal-setting exercise may become a
meaningless, empty activity* (Wolff and Astin 1990, p. 10).

Many of the faculty's "resistant" voices to assessment are
more easily understood within the critical framework offered
by Wolff.

*One problem with a linear, goal-center approach is that
it is commonly viewed as the only model of reality. We
are learning from new theories of intellectual development that there are other equally valid models of human and organizational functioning, other ways of
knowing, that can be applied to assessment* (Wolff and
Astin 1990, pp. 10–11).

Wolff suggests as one alternative goal-free models or models
that are built on inductive approaches to assessment that
generate data around questions of importance, noting that
institutional goals may in fact be derived from such a process rather than being the first step. He suggests beginning
with "critical questions" about which concern is shared and
notes that derivation of institutional goals may then be the
last, rather than the first, step in assessment, because de

facto goals may be identified through the examination of students' actual work.

Wolff's arguments for a "culture of evidence" are compatible with dynamic, systemic frameworks for understanding change. Many faculty critics of assessment have argued forcefully against simple linear concepts of change that fail to accommodate the complexity of change. Wolff suggests a model that responds to these criticisms:

> *A culture of evidence would reflect attentiveness in institutional decision making to questions, particularly questions about educational purposes, and to indicators that lead to the development of information about issues of importance to stakeholders within the institution* (Wolff and Astin 1990, p. 7).

Importantly, Wolff's position acknowledges that assessment should be tailored to answer questions of interest rather than tailoring the questions to fit the model of assessment.

Differing Disciplinary Epistemologies

Lee Shulman, professor of education at Stanford University and head of the Carnegie Foundation for the Advancement of Teaching, has noted how theorists and practitioners have gone awry separating process and content in trying to understand learning. This unfortunate separation has occurred in many different approaches to assessment of college-level learning. Naive assumptions about generic abilities that generalize across content or disciplinary areas have led to approaches to assessment that purport to be content-free. According to Shulman, if we wish to assess processes, we must embed them in content. Most research, he says, argues against the transferability of process learning from one domain to a different one—that most concepts of critical reasoning per se or higher-order thinking per se are not supported by research on human learning. Many approaches to assessment continue to presume this transferability, however.

Shulman suggests then that appropriate assessments presuppose an understanding of the kind of growth in knowledge one wishes to assess, and asserts that more scholarship must be done on the development of understanding within disciplinary specialties. He proposes, for example, longitudinal case studies of what people who are history majors learn

Naive assumptions about generic abilities that generalize across content or disciplinary areas have led to approaches to assessment that purport to be content-free.

from college, and what changes occur in what they understand in their specific subject areas as well as in their general knowledge based on taking more courses.

> *Scholarship on the development of understanding history should be done by historians as well as by psychologists who understand a lot of history. And the same is true for biology and the other fields you teach* (Shulman, Smith, and Stewart 1987, p. 13).

Shulman's views are consistent with those of many critics of assessment among the faculty, who have argued against generic, reductionist approaches to assessment. To be useful in higher education, assessment must be able to capture differences in higher-order thinking and problem solving that are grounded in disciplinary specialization.

To capture the kinds of growth in knowledge he identifies, Shulman suggests the need for a whole new generation of assessment tools and, with them, a new psychometric theory. Realizing the roles that assessment plays in shaping educational systems, he says:

> *The necessary defense of an assessment system is that demonstration that, if people take it so seriously that they redesign their curricula to meet the standards that are inherent in it, they will have done something fundamentally educative for those students* (Shulman, Smith, and Stewart 1987, p. 14).

Shulman suggests that assessment be grounded in an understanding of knowing within a discipline or other framework. Learning French feminist literary criticism is different from learning quantum physics—obvious to students if not to faculty. Meaningful assessment will capture these differences, not avoid them. "Teaching to the test" would not be problematic if tests effectively captured the kinds of learning associated with development of expertise in a discipline. It is terribly problematic, however, to teach to the test when the construction of the test does not reflect that learning. Assessment could serve to make visible the differences among (and even within) disciplines in the kinds of thinking processes that are cultivated in students. Assessment that illuminates different learning processes can play a crucial role in improving the effectiveness of those processes. Clearly, this approach to assessment fits well with the historically central role of the faculty in teaching.

Not surprisingly, faculty have generally resisted approaches to assessment that are not matched with the curricular objectives they value. These curricular objectives vary dramatically across departments and programs, and the diverse approaches to understanding and multiple perspectives on what constitutes credible evidence are at the core of university life. It is no wonder that faculty balk at assessment of the effectiveness of programs that do not capture these differences.

Shulman's challenges, however, do not invite a quick fix. He provides a clear moral mandate to engage in assessment that can adequately represent the depth and complexity of the learning processes associated with the best of higher education. The process of generating clear enough understandings about the many forms of learning within and across disciplines will require careful scholarship and reflection. Inevitably, processes akin to those involved in peer review of research must inform useful strategies for assessing the effectiveness of approaches to enhancing students' learning. Assessment that will be genuinely useful in improving curriculum and instruction must necessarily be guided by an insider's perspective on learning in a specialized area. Faculty are key to this process.

A Focus on Students and Learning Processes
Pat Hutchings, founding director of the Assessment Forum at the American Association for Higher Education (AAHE), came from the English Department at Alverno College, which, she acknowledges, was an important influence in shaping her approaches to assessment. Hutchings and her colleagues at Alverno have done more than any other individual or group to make explicit the links between assessment and learning. Their work has done much to shape the context for discussions of assessment in higher education, moving away from teachers and disembodied outcomes to a focus on students and learning processes. Hutchings's writings, in particular, have clarified a focus to an evolving definition of assessment that has shaped the national conversation in higher education.

An expanded view of assessment "continues the emphasis on outcomes but strives to get behind them, to understand how they come about" (Hutchings 1989, p. 4).

The current focus on outcomes often misses the mark when it comes to improvement. . . . Assessment focused solely on outcomes may miss what many campus practitioners are finding the most valuable about assessment: new richer conversations about educational purposes and processes (Hutchings 1989, p. 3).

It is important to know under what conditions students learn best: "Assessment 'behind outcomes' means looking more carefully at the processes and conditions that lead to the learning we care about" (p. 1). Hutchings also stressed the importance of moving beyond an exclusive focus on academic achievement to consider other aspects of students' growth and development: "Assessment needs a broader conception of learning. . . . It leaves too many important areas for growth, too many sources of potential learning unexamined" (p. 4).

Hutchings's work highlights the fit between this concept of assessment and the "natural" roles and concerns of faculty. She warns that "a sure route to nowhere is to have assessment come forward as an 'add-on' activity unrelated to the regular work of faculty and students" (Hutchings 1990b, p. 6). Clearer and deeper understandings of students' educational experiences, according to Hutchings, are prerequisite to improved outcomes. Assessment allows faculty to understand more systematically how students move through the curriculum. "Faculty ask assessment's questions because they need answers to do their daily work with students. Assessment, for faculty, means a habit of looking at teaching in terms of its effects: learning" (Hutchings 1990a, p. 14).

Hutchings has written about assessment as a mind-set rather than a set of techniques or methods, as a set of questions about student learning rather than a set of strategies for answering questions and habits of inquiry tied to a culture of evidence around student learning. Such questions impel greater self-consciousness about both purpose and practice and a willingness to change what one does based on evidence about effectiveness. "Assessment is a way of enacting a greater seriousness about teaching; it also challenges us . . . to look harder at what it would mean to be really serious about teaching" (Hutchings 1990a, p. 42). Clearly, this view of assessment involves a transformative vision; assessment becomes a project involving institutional change. The promise of assessment, as Hutchings describes it, is students' improved learning. Assessment serves a role in fostering conversations, facilitating movement in the direction of collective goals and expectations for students' learning.

The dynamic process Hutchings describes follows from the ways in which faculty think about the learning they value. Assessment calls for clearer and more public articulation of shared expectations. Thus, "assessment demands a deeper analysis and clearer account of what we expect students to 'take away' from this or that course of study" (Hutchings and Reuben 1988, p. 53). "Choices about what to assess and how to do it should be governed first and foremost by what's good for students" (Hutchings 1989, p. 30). Thus, the success of efforts to improve students' academic growth depends on the continuous availability of information.

According to Hutchings, simple, easily digestible data on outcomes rarely relate to the real concerns of faculty about students' learning. As a result, they are unlikely to lead to collective efforts to bring about improvement. Looking systematically at students' progress through the curriculum is a much more complex task.

According to Hutchings, simple, easily digestible data on outcomes rarely relate to the real concerns of faculty about students' learning. As a result, they are unlikely to lead to collective efforts to bring about improvement.

> *Using assessment to get behind outcomes means that more people, using a wide variety of methods, will look at a broader range of concerns; it means a more complex array of information that will never lend itself to neat, bottom-line scores and reports* (Hutchings 1989, p. 30).

The assessment Hutchings envisions is broadly participative and multifaceted, and captures faculty members' best collective sense of how to maximize learning for diverse groups of students.

The Tie between Assessment and Teaching Practice

In classroom assessment, individual classroom teachers are personally and intellectually involved in the assessment of students' learning in their classrooms. And the scale is very different from institutional or systemwide approaches. K. Patricia Cross, a retired professor from the University of California at Berkeley and one of the pioneers of classroom assessment, describes classroom assessment as:

> *A grassroots movement in which college teachers design the assessment measures themselves and engage in con-*

tinuous collection of information about student learning in their own classrooms. . . . The task of the classroom assessor is to continuously monitor student learning and to experiment with teaching techniques and strategies, searching for those that will improve students' learning (Cross 1990, p. 5).

A major problem of assessment

. . . is that faculty members are not fully involved in the process, and the results of the institutional assessment are rarely used to make a difference in the classroom, . . . [although] because classroom assessments are created, administered, and analyzed by teachers themselves on questions of teaching and learning that are important to them, the likelihood that instructors will apply the results of the assessments in their own teaching is greatly enhanced (Angelo and Cross 1993, pp. xiii–xiv).

This approach to assessment responds to the needs of faculty for specific, timely information about particular individuals in their classrooms.

A variety of classroom assessment techniques can be adapted to many learning contexts (see, e.g., Angelo 1994; Cross and Angelo 1988), including assessment of course-related knowledge and skills, learners' attitudes, values, and self-awareness, and learners' reactions to instruction, through minute papers, course-related self-confidence surveys, and classroom assessment quality circles. Such methods can empower both teachers and students to improve the quality of students' learning. Classroom assessment is rooted in a deep understanding and appreciation of traditional roles of faculty within the academy.

A defining characteristic of any profession is that it depends on the wise and effective use of judgment and knowledge. . . . [Classroom assessment] respects the autonomy, academic freedom, and professional judgment of college faculty. . . . The individual teacher decides what to assess, how to assess, and how to respond to the information gained through assessment (Cross and Angelo 1988, p. 4).

Both the particularity and the locality of this approach fit well with a culture that respects disciplinary differences. Sharp differences exist between classroom assessment and large-scale assessment, which is "rarely designed to ask questions that are meaningful and useful to individual classroom teachers" (Cross and Angelo 1988, p. 9). For instance, the necessary preparation and orientation to these processes of assessment are quite different:

> *Those carrying out assessment at the institutional and program levels need to be trained in research design, sampling theory, the collection and management of large pools of data, sophisticated statistical analysis, or increasingly specialized methods of qualitative research. Faculty members engaged in [classroom assessment] usually do not need these specialized research methods, because they are not required to establish publicly defensible, replicable results. Instead, they are interested in uncovering trends and indications, often of an informal nature, that can inform and improve teaching. To succeed in [classroom assessment], they need only detailed knowledge of the discipline, dedication to teaching, and the motivation to improve* (Cross and Angelo 1988, pp. 10–11).

In noting the importance of classroom assessment as a major conceptual advance in the assessment movement over time, we draw some exceptions to the clear contrasts drawn by Angelo and Cross between their approach and large-scale approaches to assessment. Just as it is the challenge of large-scale approaches to refine methods to become more meaningful and useful to individual classroom teachers, it is the challenge of practitioners of classroom assessment to refine their methods to establish their credibility and public defensibility as methods that offer promise for improving students' learning. By bringing together faculty who are involved in classroom assessment to share their findings, it becomes possible to develop a broader picture of important issues in student learning at a particular institution. By assembling the pieces of the puzzle provided by individual faculty members, the institution can identify cross-cutting issues and concerns as well as strategies that will result in improved learning for particular students. As the popularity of classroom assessment at institutions across the country already would suggest, pervasive small-scale, localized and particularized approaches to assessment may well provide the most important evidence to external constituencies calling for greater accountability—the evidence of consistent, continuing improvement of students' learning, which requires that classroom assessment be linked to broader outcomes assessment to document its effect.

The Link between Assessment and Quality Improvement
Quality improvement initiatives associated with Total Quality Management or Continuous Quality Improvement in higher education have altered both the context for assessment and the nature of the conversations about assessment on many campuses. Ted Marchese, AAHE vice president and editor of *Change* magazine, seeded many of these important discussions. Although in many ways distinct streams of reform, the quality agenda and the assessment agenda have overlapped and fertilized each other. Both reform initiatives share a commitment to operating on the basis of evidence, what quality proponents might call "management by fact," as well as a commitment to improvement. Tried and true approaches to assessment have made their way into the collection of strategies employed in association with institutional quality initiatives. Although faculty have been skeptical about the use of corporate or industrial models of management in higher education despite strong pressures on institutions to become more nimble, flexible, and adaptable to the times, these pressures propelled a great deal of the interest, particularly in administrative support areas, in the quality movement on campuses across the country. Selected elements of Total Quality Management have pervaded many components of institutional operations on many campuses, among them the University of Maryland, Central Missouri State University, and Northwest Missouri State University. Thinking associated with "quality" has enriched the frameworks in which much assessment is conducted on campuses across the country.

For example, advocates of quality initiatives think of processes that can be improved continuously rather than focus on more static concepts of goals or outcomes.

Ironically, in fact, assessment may have helped to reinforce this conservatism by reifying the notion that teaching and learning should be viewed from the perspective of a fixed set of instructional goals rather than, as was the movement's original intent, inducing ongoing examination of both goals and practices in the light of obtained results (Ewell 1993c, p. 54).

Thus, the influence of quality initiatives on assessment has brought greater attention to the dynamic elements of setting and attaining goals and an enhanced focus on continuity in assessment. As a result, assessment has come to be envisioned as a continuing agenda, rather than something to be gotten over, at many more institutions.

Similarly, quality initiatives have provided an important conceptual link between improvement of processes and improved outcomes, which has fostered greater attention to improved learning in both local and specific contexts. The quality initiative's participatory spirit of involving all who are knowledgeable about specific processes in efforts aimed at improvement has opened the way to greater faculty involvement in and claim on assessment. Conversations about effectiveness have been substantially altered by adopting this different lens on the functioning of organizations.

But the focus on customers associated with quality initiatives has been a flash point for the introduction of a quality agenda on many campuses. In particular, many faculty voice strong opposition to any attempts to identify students as customers of the institution. Some of their objections to this shift in thinking are quite persuasive, and concerns about making higher education a commodity cannot be taken lightly. For assessment and for many other functions on campus today, however, perspectives from Total Quality Management have offered the benefit of refocusing structures and processes away from the needs and preferences of faculty and staff to students and their learning.

... perspectives from Total Quality Management have offered the benefit of refocusing structures and processes away from the needs and preferences of faculty and staff to students and their learning.

Critical Voices from the Margin

Over the last 25 years, administrators and faculty in women's studies and ethnic studies and proponents of critical theory in education, among others, have offered compelling criticisms of curricula and pedagogy and the uses of assessment in colleges and universities. The criticisms have focused most acutely on issues of the distribution of power and resources and the politics surrounding decisions about what is taught, how things are taught, how decisions are made about the inclusion and exclusion of various groups from our institutions, and how standards or criteria for performance are negotiated. For many of these groups on the margin, approaches to assessment that aimed to capture dominant understandings of what it is important to know as a college or university graduate threatened even greater marginalization. They offered persistent reminders that assessment is neither value-free nor value-neutral.

Michael Nettles, professor of education and public policy at the University of Michigan, edited two volumes dealing with the effects of assessment on minority students' participation in higher education (Nettles 1990; Nettles and Nettles 1995), providing insightful analyses about how assessment can and has been used to screen out minority students as well as how it can be used to assist minority students, and how much more research on assessment is needed to understand its effects on minority students. Nettles observed, for example, that assessment can assist minority students when tests are used not simply as screening devices, but also as aids in designing interventions to help students learn and acquire the knowledge and skills they need.

Researchers on assessment should consider several important questions:

> *Are minority students attaining the goals and objectives that our assessment programs are measuring? Are these students reaching the competencies that institutions define as measures of success? Which assessment instruments are appropriate for minorities? Under which assessment alternatives are minorities successful?* (Garcia 1990, p. 73).

This same volume offers an important twist on the usual understandings of assessment (D. Smith 1990). For example, assessment can play an important role in gauging an institution's readiness for diversity. Understanding the institutional factors associated with the success of minority students, rather than simply focusing on students' characteristics, is likely to enhance progress toward greater diversity (D. Smith 1990).

The most influential volume on feminist assessment, *Students at the Center* (Musil 1992), is a report of a FIPSE-supported collaboration focused on feminist assessment. Though the intent of this volume was to provide a useful framework for assessing women's studies programs, the recommendations for assessment that were offered apply to a much broader context and added substantially to a broader national conversation about assessment.

> *We begin by assuming that what has been done before probably is inadequate—and often inadequate because it has not posed enough questions to see power relations, to note who is missing from the discussion, to appreciate the importance of context, and to understand the need to cross paradigms or to recognize shifting paradigms for purposes of assessment* (Shapiro 1992, p. 31).

Many of the principles identified as consistent with a feminist approach to assessment address concerns of broader faculty constituencies about typical assessment practices. With regard to forging broad generalities:

> *Feminist assessment recognizes there is no single student who can possibly stand for the whole. In keeping with its theoretical suspicion of aggregates and universals that too often have obscured women as a group or women in our particularity—such as women of color, women with disabilities, older women, or lesbians—feminist assessment pays attention to the distinctiveness of the individual learner. It also looks for possible and more informative patterns emerging from smaller disaggregate groupings. Since the standpoint from which each of us views the world leads inevitably toward partial perspectives, feminist assessment gains its power from holding on as much as possible to the insights of those partial perspectives, forming in the process a more textured and collective whole* (Shapiro 1992, pp. 31–32).

Feminist approaches to assessment that rely on participatory processes challenge traditional hierarchical patterns and power relationships.

> *Grounded in feminist theory—which seeks to understand oppressive silencing—and in feminist pedagogy— which seeks to give students voice—feminist assessment is deeply committed to an interactive strategy that generates a rich conversation. Less like an external process*

imposed by detached and distanced experts, feminist
assessment resembles more a group of people gathered
together to create meaning. As such, it opens up the
process rather than narrowing its options and opinions
(Shapiro 1992, p. 32).

Feminist approaches also emphasize the importance of context or institutional culture, avoiding "abstractions that are
not understood to be firmly rooted in a specific time, place,
or history" (p. 32). Issues of position or perspective are also
important, as feminist assessment attempts to decenter authority. Relationships shape both the questions asked and
the methods pursued.

> *Feminist assessment begins to deconstruct the usual*
> *"outside-in" or stringent vertical hierarchy to create a*
> *more open, varied, and weblike structure. It avoids an*
> *"outsider" or more dominant, powerful, and seemingly*
> *objective force determining what questions should be*
> *asked and how they should be framed. It also avoids an*
> *attempt to meet some abstract notion of excellence that*
> *has no roots or connection to the group, program, or*
> *curriculum being evaluated* (Shapiro 1992, p. 33).

The focus on inside-out rather than outside-in means that
neutrality is not a desired role for the assessor. "Feminist
assessment begins with and enacts values" (Shapiro 1992, p.
35). The commitment to social activism in feminist assessment leads to an understanding of methods of assessment as
ways to give voice to those who otherwise might not be
heard. Rather than identifying assessment as another irrele-
vant bureaucratic process, practitioners of feminist assessment would see their methods as instruments of change.

At least one feminist model of assessment is quite congenial
to many faculty members' understanding of their proper role:

> *In its best form, assessment contributes to the life of the*
> *academy in a way that promotes further thought, inter-*
> *personal and professional connections, and enhanced*
> *student development opportunities. To begin any assess-*
> *ment project is to enter into a conversation about all*
> *the important issues in education: What are we hoping*
> *students learn (goals)? How do we arrange things so*

they learn that (curriculum, pedagogy, requirements)?
Do we think it's happening, and, if not, how might it
happen better (evaluation)? (Tarule and Tetreault 1992,
pp. 49–50).

Many of the observations on "feminist assessment" are
broadly applicable to assessment practice and contribute
to understandings of assessment that are much more congenial to faculty.

Likewise, critical theorist William Tierney envisions an
important role for assessment in a changed culture in the
academy, advocating movement away from the current culture of the isolation of individuals that so characterizes higher
education. He envisions an important role for assessment in a
new climate of encouragement rather than fear in the academy. "If academe is a community, then we need to focus on
how assessment is an ongoing developmental activity" (Tierney 1998, p. 55). The faculty's role in assessment is trans-
formed fundamentally in this new vision of the academy.

> *Reflexive assessment moves away from a culture of fear*
> *and retribution and toward an understanding of how*
> *to create a climate for improvement. In effect, I am sug-*
> *gesting that rather than develop an evaluation system*
> *that looks backward and determines how well someone*
> *performed, we create a structure that looks forward*
> *and tries to outline how the individual and organiza-*
> *tion want to perform* (Tierney 1998, p. 55).

This encouraging, optimistic call for cultural transformation
positions faculty very differently in their relationships to one
another and to their institutions. And assessment in this context becomes a cooperative, affirming enterprise.

The enumeration of conceptual advances in assessment in
this section has identified broad ways of thinking about assessment or orientations to the task that offer promise for
fundamentally revisioning the enterprise and having it become more consistent with traditional faculty roles in the
academy. Each changing framework—the development of
students, a move away from assuring minimal competency,
going beyond linear, goal-centered approaches, taking note
of epistemological differences among the disciplines, students and their learning processes, the relationship between

*William
Tierney en-
visions an
important
role for as-
sessment in
a changed
culture in
the acad-
emy, advo-
cating move-
ment away
from the
current
culture of
the isolation
of individu-
als that so
character-
izes higher
education.*

assessment and teaching practice, thinking of improvement as a continuing agenda, attending to critical voices from the margin—offers a vision of assessment that is congenial to traditional faculty values and sensibilities. Clearly the understandings of what we are about in assessment have changed dramatically in the past decade—as have methodological frameworks.

METHODOLOGICAL ADVANCES

Focusing on faculty's reaction to various approaches to the assessment of students' learning, this section traces a shift away from broad-scale standardized testing to more locally developed approaches to assessment that are more congruent with faculty values. After critiquing national, mass-market, generic assessment instruments for their inability to provide information faculty find valid and valuable, the section identifies several innovations in assessment that lead to a more complex understanding of academic work today while still honoring traditional faculty values and mores: (1) fitting measurement to a local context, (2) seeking convergence among multiple measures, (3) involving new disciplinary perspectives, (4) valuing authenticity, and (5) distinguishing between measurement and judgment.

Testing in a Local Context

Both the history of assessment in the K–12 sector and the prominence and entrepreneurial interest of a uniquely American testing industry influenced the character of many of the first assessment programs in the recent wave of assessment in higher education. During the 1970s, concerns about the quality of elementary and secondary education moved the issue of quality of the schools into the political arena in many locales. Testing for proficiency was posed as a solution to this problem. Currently, 45 states have statewide assessment programs, and two others have temporarily suspended their assessment systems as they design new ones (North Central 1996).

Over time, broad-scale standardized testing became the mode of assessment most commonly used in the K–12 sector, although recently a broader range of approaches is being used. A 1996 survey indicates that the number of states reporting the use of multiple-choice instruments is approximately equal to the number using non-multiple-choice instruments, and that the number using norm-referenced tests is approximately equal to those using criterion-referenced tests (North Central 1996). Calls for assessment of the effectiveness of higher education, not surprisingly, initially provoked suggestions to go with "grown-up" versions of the standardized tests used in the K–12 sector. A very successful, entrepreneurial, multimillion dollar testing industry seemed poised to take on this new challenge. Over time, however, a great deal of criticism has surrounded proposals for the use of such strategies to assess the effectiveness of institutions of higher education. Admittedly, simply taking something off the shelf is initially appealing. Responding to external calls for accountability by designating someone in an office of institutional research or a testing center to test a group of students using an available standardized measure seemed an easy solution to "the problem." Students could be tested, scores could be reported, and faculty could continue their work without missing a beat. In fact, the majority of faculty have assumed that calls for accountability are most appropriately answered in this way.

But some faculty from early in the assessment movement came to identify potential threats to their control over the curriculum by the use of standardized testing to assess effectiveness. Specifically,

> *A heavy emphasis on uniform tests threatens to trivialize undergraduate teaching and to rob it of diversity by orienting instruction too heavily toward a single imperfect means of measurement. Such a policy will not interest the faculty, let alone the abler students, and hence will not encourage a broad-based effort to enhance the quality of education* (Bok 1986, p. 59).

The AAUP's statement on mandated assessment notes, "Those standardized measurement instruments that are the easiest to replicate are the least valid in any context other than the assessment of basic skills" (American Association 1991, p. 52). Committee C argues that, as a result of mandated assessment, changes in the curriculum will occur to emphasize what is "measurable," which will necessarily mean greater emphasis on developing skills to the exclusion of learning values. Further, diverse institutional missions and curricular approaches across institutions result in little commonality in the experiences of college students. On most college and university campuses, for example, faculty spend considerable time and energy debating the goals, content, and structure of general education curricula—that component of coursework at the institution shared by all students, regardless of major or emphasis. These discussions often begin with a focus on the distinct mission and character of the institution and the unique aspirations of faculty for their particular group of students (Project 1994). Both the architecture of these curricula and the content areas represented vary considerably across institutions (Gaff 1991; Spear, Ferren, and Romano 1992).

Further complicating this picture is the fact that distributional models of general education are far more common at institutions today than are core curricular models that prescribe a common set of courses for all students. Ninety-three percent of all general education programs are of the course distribution type (Hurtado, Astin, and Dey 1991). Thus, even within a particular institution, students may take very different selections of courses to satisfy a general education requirement.

These differences among students' course selections are then further amplified quite dramatically by choice of major. Beyond the already divergent paths pursued in completing general education requirements, the likely overlap in courses taken between, say, an English literature major and a chemistry major is quite small.

Yet broad-scale standardized testing necessarily begins with assumptions about the existence of commonality. Test design is based on sampling from a presumed shared universe of items representing materials students have learned. Standardized tests of general education outcomes, such as ACT-COMP, Academic Profile, and College BASE, thus sample from a presumed common range of content and processes.

To assess competencies in an area such as social sciences, several items are chosen for inclusion. In many distributional models of general education, social science may include anthropology, sociology, psychology, political science, economics, and geography. So a version of the test in a particular year may include a few items that sample content from sociology, a few that sample content from psychology, and a few that sample content from political science. For students who completed this component of their requirements by taking anthropology, economics, or geography, this test quite obviously may not provide a good index of the curriculum's effectiveness in social science—particularly if questions emphasize, as is often the case, mastery of content rather than cross-cutting reasoning processes in the social sciences. Similarly, emphases of courses developed specifically to meet specific curricular objectives may not be represented at all in this more generic approach to assessment. A distinctive mission or unique curricular goals are necessarily a wash in these generic approaches to assessment.

Profiles of the performance of students at one institution compared with students at "similar" institutions may be available as a result of this form of assessment. This kind of profile, on the surface, may seem particularly useful in satisfying calls for accountability. But faculty ask, wisely, what the tests measure. They also question the usefulness of cross-institutional comparisons of this sort (American Association 1991).

Further, generic measures that are not related to agreed-upon specific curricular objectives are rarely seen by the faculty as having much relevance to their teaching or curricular decision making. Rather than being seen as simply not useful or unrelated to institutional curricular objectives and instruction, such tests have tended to generate skepticism or cynicism among many faculty, who fear that focus on test scores in a comparative framework almost always provokes the response of teaching to the test. That is, they fear that concern with test results subverts the proper role of the faculty in curricular decision making by driving faculty to attend more carefully to materials that are to be tested than to the materials they and their colleagues have used their professional judgments to select. Teaching to the test need not be seen as a problem if the measure used effectively captures success in attaining identified objectives, which will only rarely be the case for most widely used standardized tests of outcomes of higher education.

Scores on standardized measures of general education outcomes designed for broad-scale use typically correlate at a quite significant level with scores on college entrance examinations and other standardized measures of achievement. Thus, cross-institutional comparisons do not simply tell a story about the curriculum's effectiveness. Rather, these scores may tell much more about students' entry-level abilities. Similar results have been observed on standardized tests in the major field (Nowaczyk and Frey 1982). On the Graduate Record Examination advanced test in psychology, for example, performance was more affected ($r = .65$) by students' SAT scores than by any other measures, including GPA ($r = .44–.49$) or hours of psychology courses completed ($r = .30$).

A comparison of the relative merits of several standardized measures of general education outcomes for indexing gains at Miami University, part of a FIPSE-supported project, involved administering the ACT-COMP and the Academic Profile to graduating seniors. An initial reading of results showed a very high level of performance among students (and by association for the curriculum and instructors), but testing entering students on these same measures provided some important, though humbling, insights. For the typical highly able student admitted to Miami University, it was common to score near the ceiling on these measures in the entry-level assessment. These measures, then, were of little use in indexing gains related to the curriculum over four years. At best, they might demonstrate that students were not harmed by the curriculum.

Similarly, institutions with a mission to serve at-risk students may find their accomplishments with students poorly represented by below-average scores on these measures, despite the fact that other dramatic evidence suggests students' gains. Using an intrainstitutional framework and testing students with measures that are clearly linked to curricular objectives at both entry and exit may demonstrate impressive curricular outcomes. Yet cross-institutional comparisons using these same data interpreted by using available norms for a broad range of institutions may be quite demoralizing for the faculty, demonstrating students' below-average performance at the time of exit.

None of these criticisms identify inherent faults with standardized testing. Rather, they identify problems in the use of broad-scale standardized testing to answer specific questions or provide data on the effectiveness of colleges and universities. When there is a high degree of agreement about curricular goals, as is the case for particular segments of the K–12 experience, then using tests that index this curricular commonality and provide cross-institutional normative information is not only an efficient, but also an effective approach to assessment. Absent this commonality, however, it is difficult for average faculty members to find anything useful in broad-scale standardized test results for improving their daily work with students or for revising the curriculum.

Many institutions have turned to locally developed measures because of these concerns with broad-scale standardized testing. And they have found that local curricular commitments can be much more faithfully mirrored in items developed by faculty who share an understanding of an institution's curricular goals. Although the development of test instruments is expensive and measures specific to one institution do not provide useful normative data across institutions, better indices of the effectiveness of institutions in meeting specific missions and goals can be developed when a much narrower context for assessment is identified. Such measures have much greater potential for embodying local culture in terms of agreed-upon expectations for students' learning. The process of test development itself requires that faculty engage in conversations about common goals, and such conversations encourage the faculty's authority over the curriculum and its assessment. As a result, faculty are much more likely to take ownership of test results, and they are far less likely to reflexively dismiss the results because of items' perceived idiosyncrasies or peculiarities. For all of these reasons, test results from locally developed measures are far more likely to be perceived as relevant to curricular decision making and to have far greater synergy with curricular planning. They are thus much more likely to be tied to improvement of the curriculum.

Multiple Measures of Performance
Although too easy to caricature, many faculty would see their proper role as making the simple more complex—introducing subtleties and nuances into what on the surface may seem simple and straightforward. Thus, it is easy to understand why one of the faculty's greatest concerns about assessment is that approaches chosen will be reductionist—that the full complexity of what they do will not be faithfully represented by the data presented. From this perspective, the most important questions of many faculty about assessment really are questions of validity: Does this measure relate in any way to what I do? Over time, successful attempts at assessment have recognized the aversion of faculty to reductionism and have tried to accommodate the complexity of the enterprise. One important step in this direction has been the advocacy of the use of multiple measures of performance rather than reliance on single indices. Use of multiple measures clearly adds to the credibility of assessment results among the faculty.

Assessment measures are used to provide indications of mastery or understanding. For many of the complex skills and abilities that would be associated with college-level work, simple and direct indicators are not available. Constructs like critical thinking have multiple levels of meaning that require complex models of interpretation. For example, a report on consensus or agreement among faculty employers and policy makers on understandings of critical thinking and several other skills noted, with regard to critical thinking,

> . . . *students need to determine [whether] arguments rest*
> *on false, biased, or doubtful assumptions; evaluate the*
> *credibility, accuracy, and reliability of sources of infor-*
> *mation; assess the importance of an argument and deter-*
> *mine [whether] it merits attention; evaluate an argument*
> *in terms of reasonability and practicality; assess statistical*
> *information; determine how new data may lead to fur-*
> *ther confirmation or questioning of a conclusion; deter-*
> *mine [whether] conclusions are derived from sufficiently*
> *large and representative samples; and evaluate analogies*
> (Jones, Hoffman, Moore, Ratcliff, Tibbetts, and Click
> 1994, p. 40).

From this complex, operational definition of critical thinking, it is clear that most faculty (and perhaps employers and policy makers if prodded to reflect more deeply) will reject a simple operationalization of this or similar constructs. They find approaches like "triangulation" (Merriam 1988), that is, looking at patterns of convergence among different measures that attempt to capture related elements of a construct, much more intellectually satisfying and interpreting the patterns of results (as opposed to finding an answer in a simple result) consistent with their understanding of higher-order thinking. Faculty are trained to be cautious in their assertions about findings, and making broad claims for effectiveness based on one measure is inconsistent with their general dispositions. Striving to make sense of divergent patterns of evidence resulting from the use of multiple measures inspires appropriate humility about capacities to assess complex constructs related to higher-order learning. It can provide a helpful reminder of what is "higher" about higher education.

Many different epistemologies or theories of learning and knowing are found in institutions of higher education. Some would argue that it is the richness of these very differences among disciplinary and other approaches to knowing that makes a college or university. The important differences are not just that physicists do physics and literary scholars do literature, but that physicists approach their world and problem solving in ways that differ from the approaches literary scholars use. They may also hold different views of what constitutes adequate evidence. Approaches to assessment that rely on multiple measures are more likely to accommodate these important disciplinary differences. In making visible the differences in strategies, approaches, goals, and so on across and even within some disciplines, assessment that relies on multiple measures promotes dialogue and explicitly evokes discussions of values and priorities related to students' learning. Multiple measures are useful in moving these conversations away from silence or dualistic, good-bad debates about quality to conversations about shared goals and objectives and unique contributions of different units to students' overall development. The use of one metric suggests the operation of only one paradigm. The use of multiple measures, however, enhances opportunities for recognizing varied instructional paradigms. Humanities scholars may have very little interest in means and standard deviations on some quantitative measure of student outcomes, but they may be quickly persuaded of the utility of some qualitative or ethnographic approach to understanding curricular impact. Engineers, on the other hand, may be more easily persuaded by quantitative indices. When multiple measures are employed, conversations may bridge some of these disciplinary differences.

By using different approaches to or measures of assessment, it is also easier to capture the complexity of and differences among students' learning styles and to provide evidence that is consistent with multivariate concepts of students' growth and development. Multiple measures offer the promise of capturing the complex multidimensionality of both the curriculum and students' performance, of creating a picture of day-to-day life in the academy that captures some of the complexity that faculty expect to see in any realistic depiction of their daily challenges.

Beyond the Psychometricians
Much of the early work in assessment relied on the development of standardized tests and surveys (see, e.g., Pace 1979). Considerable expertise from education and psychology informed this developing practice in assessment. Experts in measurement worked closely with specialists in varied fields to provide strategies that would yield both reliable and valid summative indicators of performance on clearly identified constructs. Corporations like the Educational Testing Service

Humanities scholars may have very little interest in means and standard deviations on some quantitative measure of student outcomes, but they may be quickly persuaded of the utility of some qualitative or ethnographic approach to understanding curricular impact.

brought together immensely talented experts in measurement to develop measures for an impressive variety of fields. Beyond these large-scale approaches to standardized testing, several campuses across the country also assembled impressive local expertise to develop campus-based measures. At Alverno College, the University of Tennessee, and Kean College of New Jersey, for example, considerable technical assistance in the construction and evaluation of tests was provided to assist faculty in their attempts to develop local measures of outcomes for various campus programs.

Sophisticated and highly differentiated models of the validity of measurement have evolved over time. In fact, in many areas, the sophistication of and technologies involved in measurement have outstripped the clarity of thinking about constructs to be measured. Critics have written of the "methodolotry" associated with this rise of operationalism in American psychology. The dominant belief was that if something exists it can be measured. In fact, many faculty fear the embodiment of the obverse of this statement in actual practice, as constructs appear to be "realized" through measurement. Faculty members' goals and objectives in their teaching are often more diffuse and unspecified than available measurement technologies might suggest. Faculty who are tentative about stating goals and objectives for fear that such statements may constrain their behavior may be wary of methods through which the signifier might become the signified. Further, many faculty resist the overall framework of mental measurement underlying these approaches to assessment. And they are particularly suspicious of the apparent precision brought to what they see as an imprecise enterprise.

Further, faculty argue that the investment of considerable time and resources on any campus to develop reliable and valid measures may introduce untoward pressures not to change courses, curricula, and instructional methods. The very investment of energy in perfecting measures of the way things are done currently may serve to discourage curricular innovation. Committee C's report on mandated assessment notes that "reliable comparisons between disparate programs, or within individual programs over time, demand narrow and unchanging instruments, and thus may discourage necessary curricular improvement and variety" (American Association 1991, p. 55). The more comprehensive and effective the approach to assessment, the less likely faculty may be to upset the apple cart by suggesting changes in the curriculum.

Not surprisingly, faculty are easily persuaded by methods akin to their disciplinary backgrounds and traditions and driven more by questions of substance within their disciplines than by the imposed methods of assessment that come from education and social science. Based on a decade of assessment in Virginia,

> . . . *faculty, like many others, will accept the results of studies most readily if they gather the data themselves, especially if the data are about their department or unit. Consequently, faculty ownership of data is one of the most important factors in the success of assessment. It is better to have less-than-perfect data gathered by departmental faculty than perfect data from some other source. Only when they trust the veracity of the data are faculty likely to act on the implications* (Muffo 1996, p. 1).

Faculty also observe that measures of course or program goals or outcomes often do not effectively capture the aspects of their involvement with students that they value most. Many faculty seem to value what would be termed "process indicators" rather than measures of goals or outcomes. The kind of information faculty seek that relates to the improvement of teaching is often of a much more formative, rather than summative, nature. Quality initiatives in higher education have borrowed from industry the notion that it is important to deliver information "just in time" for needed midcourse corrections to occur. Many faculty see formative rather than summative assessments of effectiveness as more useful in improving students' learning.

Faculty who taught writing were among the first to offer serious challenges to the lock on assessment held by the psychometricians and educational measurement people. Without invoking a great deal of the social scientific paradigm, they observed considerable consistency among colleagues in the evaluation of students' writing. Moreover, they found that holistic approaches to scoring were much more compatible with their professional judgments of quality than were approaches that involved atomistic grading of individual sentences and grammatical constructions. Likewise, faculty in the fine and performing arts brought their own distinct perspectives on evaluating quality to discussions of assessment. Remarkable successes with professional jurying of performances and portfolios of works completed and numerous other distinct traditions for judging the quality of a program have broadened understandings of needed backgrounds to engage the issue of assessment.

Authentic Approaches to Assessment

Critics of traditional approaches to assessment argue that the chosen approaches to assessment exert a strong influence on teaching and learning (see, e.g., Wiggins 1990). Standardized testing and other "efficient" systems of evaluation that rely on proxy measures of students' learning may in fact undermine efforts to enhance their learning (Wiggins 1990). "What we assess is what we value. We get what we assess, and if we don't assess it, we won't get it" (p. 20). In the search for what is efficient and what is easy to score, many strategies of assessment have ignored what is essential. Wiggins advocates the use of "authentic assessments," those comprising "tasks that we value." Such measures "should reveal something not only about the student but about the tasks and virtues at the heart of the subject—its standards" (p. 20). They are standard-setting as well as standard-revealing—as well as more engaging of students. Simulations, case studies, portfolios, and the like are much more likely to embody the kinds of learning valued by the faculty. They are not quickly summarized and easily reduced because they attempt to capture complex processes.

> *Authentic tests are more appropriately public, involving an actual audience, client, panel, and so on. The evaluation is typically based on judgment that involves multiple criteria . . . , and the judging is made reliable by agreed-upon standards and prior training.*
> *Authentic tests require some collaboration with others. . . . Authentic tests recur, and they are worth practicing, rehearsing, and retaking. . . . Feedback to students is central. . . . [And] authentic tests are not needlessly intrusive, arbitrary, or contrived merely for the sake of shaking out a single score or grade. Instead, they are "enabling"—constructed to point the student toward more sophisticated and effective ways to use knowledge.*

*Authentic tests are contextualized, complex intellec-
tual challenges, not fragmented and static bits or tasks*
(Wiggins 1989, p. 711).

Over the years, an extensive literature has developed on
strategies to motivate students to complete many of the standardized tests and other measures used in campus assessment
programs. This discussion of incentives, requirements, penal-
ties for noncompletion, and so on only thinly veils the problem of many students' unwillingness to complete measures
that have been used commonly to assess student outcomes.
This resistance on the part of students to many traditional
approaches to assessment raises serious questions about the
validity of many of the findings based on use of these measures, and suggests the wisdom of employing approaches that
are more congenial to students' sensibilities. Assessment of
students' habits and repertoires that uses portfolios, simulations, case studies, performances, and so on most often is
embedded in existing courses or programs of instruction,
rather than added to the work of professors or students.

A Clear Distinction between
Measurement and Judgment

Of the numerous options available for program assessment,
faculty still overwhelmingly identify peer review as the pre-
ferred approach to evaluating effectiveness (Banta 1995). A
contextualized judgment of quality made by a professional
with credibility in the field of focus will likely persuade faculty more than any score on a measure of adequacy of performance. As ideas of what constitutes credible evidence in
an assessment program have expanded to include not only
quantitative approaches, but also a broad range of qualitative approaches, complex interpretations of multidimensional patterns of evidence have superseded narrower and
more dualistic determinations of adequacy of performance.
Burgeoning literatures on narrative and hermeneutic research methods in a variety of humanities and social science
disciplines have enriched this discussion. Critical theorists in
education and other fields (see, e.g., Tierney 1989) have exploded assumptions of agreed-upon curricular goals and
shared criteria for excellent performance. Thus, simple, almost automated, responses to measures of effectiveness
rarely are seen by faculty as adequate substitutes for in-

formed professional judgments. New emphases on contexts and context-embedded performance as well as recognition of important differences among faculty perspectives on the precise meaning of any performance have moved understandings of assessment from tasks involving simple measurement to tasks involving complex judgments.

> *Faculty can remain sensitive to various manifestations of performance in context, avoid creating a "sea of criteria," and develop a basis for similarity in judgment and understanding. Pushing for measurement properties often did not make sense in this integrated performance assessment context* (Rogers 1994, p. 7).

Cherished traditions of peer review in academe rely on the exercise of informed, contextualized professional judgment. All indications are that assessment based in this tradition will be much more acceptable to faculty then any other approach to assessment.

Thus, the nature of assessment practice has also changed dramatically over the past 10 years. The best of contemporary practice is more richly variegated, complex, and multi-layered. It is grounded and contextualized in an understanding of teaching and learning. It is broadly participative, including representatives from a broad variety of disciplines. It is humbler in its claims of what it measures and how generalizable its results are. It is focused on the learner, and it relies on a seemingly ever-expanding set of activities. Not only have the "what" and "how" of assessment practices in higher education changed dramatically over the past decade; substantial changes have also occurred in the "why" of assessment—those very important issues having to do with the policy and politics of our institutions.

POLICY ADVANCES

This section identifies changes or trends over time in assessment policy and the politics surrounding assessment that have led, or might lead, to increased effectiveness or the acceptance of assessment among faculty at various institutions of higher education. Some faculty admittedly would think of "advances in assessment policy or politics" as oxymoronic, and the only possible advance for this group would be full-scale retreat from assessment on our campuses. And, in fact, some faculty continue to wait for the disappearance of assessment from campus agenda, viewing assessment as a passing fad to be weathered like other proposed changes they have seen come and go. This section, however, makes the case that faculty will likely become involved in assessment when institutional leaders adopt meaningful strategies that reflect institutional values and traditions.

It is important, in tracing changes in assessment over time, to distinguish between two traditions: (1) assessment that has been internally driven and related to curricular reform and pedagogical improvement; and (2) assessment that has been externally driven and related fundamentally to concerns about accountability. The interaction between the two, beginning in the 1980s and continuing to the present day, is a strange dance involving tension over states' "making" universities do things that were supposed to be so good for them (Ewell 1997).

Changing Notions of Accountability

Changing concepts of the public purposes of higher education have had enormous implications for the course of assessment (Ewell 1997). Higher education has experienced transitions in understandings of accountability from "how we do our business, to how well we do our business, to what we actually do." The dominant model, dating from the late 1960s and early 1970s, was to see public higher education as a public utility, with its primary benefit in the provision of individual goods. These goods included social mobility and the ability to get a job, among others. The associated social contract involved providing access to these private benefits, regardless of an individual's background or circumstances (Ewell 1997).

In the 1980s, a "corporatist" model was layered on this earlier understanding. In this model, higher education was viewed as a directed collective investment. The focus was on

Higher education has experienced transitions in understandings of accountability from "how we do our business, to how well we do our business, to what we actually do."

higher education as a public good, and the government had something to say about how and how well universities were doing their business. Outcomes and results thus became the focus. With legitimization of the government's steering of higher education, established through performance funding and the government's practice of looking at the academic business of higher education in the early 1990s, a second major shift in understanding of the public purposes of higher education occurred between 1992 and 1994 (Ewell 1997). This shift was back to a notion of higher education as largely a private benefit. The dominant logic of disinvestment under this model led to reductions in the public's investment share in higher education and a retreat from commitments to equity and access. And with this shift has come (1) an increasing emphasis on funding narrow forms of performance, for example, in selective payment for state priorities through performance indicator systems; (2) a growing emphasis on consumer information and marketplace mechanisms in accountability; and (3) some reemergence of statewide testing requirements. The assessment dance has changed over time, then, from policy makers' initial interest, which converged more with the faculty's potential interest in improvement, to state policy makers' interest in quality assurance.

Assessment currently is not high on the federal agenda, and a great deal of uncertainty and variability in assessment policy exists at the state level. As virtually all accreditation agencies now require assessment and other items of importance have emerged on the public radar screen, policy makers may be shifting their attention to other issues. But results-oriented policy makers' new interest in what ought to be taught and how it should be taught suggests the possibility of policy makers' greater intrusion into business as usual on college and university campuses. History suggests that faculty will be slow to respond to such intrusions, even if the stakes are high.

The Move to Performance Indicators

"Institutional assessment without a link to funding had only limited success and was not as far-reaching as policy makers desired or anticipated" (Gaither, Nedwek, and Neal 1994, p. 4). Linking assessment to incentives seemed to provide important leverage. In 1984, the Tennessee legislature put in place a goal-oriented performance funding model for its state university system. Budgetary incentives were tied to achieving desired student outcomes. By 1997, 25 states had systems of performance indicators driving models of funding for higher education (Ewell 1997). In South Carolina, for example, a model has been approved that will potentially use 37 performance indicators to determine the full allocation of resources to public higher education. Performance funding provides a vehicle for new kinds of external quality assurance at the state level, as legislators increasingly are committing themselves to paying for only what they like and want in higher education. A performance indicator is:

> . . . a concrete piece of information about a condition or result of public action that is regularly produced, publicly reported, and systematically used for planning, monitoring, or resource allocation at the state or system level. . . . [They are] intended to be used together, not singly or out of context (Ewell and Jones 1994, p. 7).

"They are often also designed, however, to influence universities' and colleges' priorities and their achievement of their mission as teachers of undergraduates" (Gaither, Nedwek, and Neal 1994, p. 2). Indicators of all sorts have been put in place, with a great deal of imitation occurring across state systems, often without appropriate consideration of reliability and validity of the identified measures (Gaither, Nedwek, and Neal 1994). Additionally, many of the performance indicators that are currently in use are input rather than outcome variables. Performance indicators will be useful to faculty insofar as they provide information related to students' learning, but unfortunately, a number of current models rely upon those data that are available rather than those that are important.

Faculty resist the drive to compare that is key to the use of performance indicators. They also strongly resist this approach when it is used to redistribute existing resources rather than to guide distribution of additional resources as incentives. Moreover, it is not clear that the underlying approach to offering "collective rewards" is effective in motivating faculty.

> While it is not easy to implement a quality and incentive program with performance indicators that actually work, a key is to develop a program based on incentives

*that are meaningful to individuals, not solely to an
institution* (Gaither, Nedwek, and Neal 1994, p. 26).

Additionally, "the goals of faculty and the state legislature
often appear at odds, almost guaranteeing some level of
ongoing tension and conflict between these groups" (p. 46),
but increasing emphasis from the states on bureaucratic accountability rather than professional accountability would
perhaps help ease the tension.

> *Current incentives provided to faculty do not encourage
> collective responsibility for quality in the academy. The
> faculty will use data from performance indicators but
> only when more incentives exist for doing so. The best
> potential for professional accountability might be through
> revisiting performance standards within the academy.
> Decisions about rank and tenure, for example, that are
> more sensitive to the heightened interest in excellent
> teaching of undergraduates could help restore more faith
> and trust in the academy for students and other con-
> sumers* (Gaither, Nedwek, and Neal 1994, pp. 85-86).

If performance indicators are to serve a useful function in
ensuring the excellence of academic programs, faculty will
need to be involved in identifying and developing appropriate measures. Such involvement to date has been limited.
Although, as noted earlier, 25 states are using performance
indicators in funding higher education, most faculty on campuses in most of those states would be unable to identify
the indicators that are currently being used. If faculty are
unaware of performance objectives, it is difficult to believe
that this approach to assessment will result in significant
change in educational practices over time.

Barriers to the Institutionalization of Assessment
The course traveled by the assessment movement on campuses over the past years has by no means been smooth
and steadily onward and upward. After more than 15 years
of activity, almost all institutions claim that they are doing
assessment, but few campuses have truly institutionalized it.

> *While it is true that assessment has been a transforming
> lever at a few colleges and universities—among them,*

Alverno, Northeast Missouri State University, and King's College—that short list hasn't grown much longer in the last few years. On most campuses, assessment efforts have resulted in a little tinkering around the edges, at best (Angelo 1996, pp. 3-4).

The problem with assessment has been the absence of an associated commitment to explicit, shared, high standards for the quality of students' learning (Angelo 1996). Without this link, assessment will have minimal impact on institutions.

Another impediment to institutionalizing assessment has been the absence of a vision.

> *Assessment has failed to inspire faculty with its transformational possibilities. I fear we have neglected the vision of assessment and trivialized the movement by talking so much about techniques. As a result, we have lost the grand vision of assessment that could inspire the faculty and win their enthusiastic support. Faculty must see assessment as a movement not as a method. What faculty need is a great cause and too often we have given them statistical techniques. Assessment must be viewed as transformational by faculty if it is to become truly operational on our campuses* (Burke 1994, p. 3).

On few campuses has any vision of the potential contributions of assessment been shared with the faculty. Most faculty cannot understand how this "new" form of data collection would be any different from all the data collection they had been part of for years. Many faculty believe that they rarely received adequate answers to the questions of "why more?" and "why now?" and "how will this be any different?"

False Starts Incurring Hostility

With the benefit of 20/20 hindsight, we can identify many things that could have been done differently to ensure more adequate institutionalization of assessment on campus. It may seem easy in retrospect to understand how a contracting resource base to support higher education would bring concerns about effectiveness and calls for accountability. Among many faculty, however, calls for accountability and the related campus focus on assessment appeared as new, unwanted, and incomprehensible burdens. Faculty wanted to know why, if the concern being voiced was about quality of instruction, resources that could ease an unmanageable instructional burden were being devoted to assessment rather than to the direct improvement of instruction. And they wanted to know how assessment was in any obvious way related to improvement. Assessment might be used to "prove," but it was not at all clear to the typical faculty member how assessment was related to "improvement."

In an era when the mantra "do more with less" guided decision making on campus, a great deal of cynicism surrounded campus conversations about accountability. "Do more with less" was not received simply as an innocent call for greater efficiency. Faculty read the subtext of this directive as a criticism of their work. "There is an antifaculty odor behind some of the public expectancy for assessment. It is connected with faculty workload legislation, with the public demanding that the people who are laboring hardest make a dysfunctional system work for students" (Marchese 1994, p. 6). Others have seen links between assessment and post-tenure review, assuming that these processes share an inimical view of the work of typical faculty members (American Association 1991). Even for those for whom the idea of assessment might not have provoked initial negativism, the idea of doing yet another "good thing" seemed oppressive. Faculty facing contracting resources and increasing burdens are unlikely to identify the opportunities in assessment. According to the AAUP's Committee C, "self-examination is best conducted in a climate free of external constraint or threats, however vaguely disguised" (American Association 1991, p. 54).

Higher education contains little, if any, history of successful top-down initiatives, as faculty ownership is a key element of change in institutions of higher education. Yet assessment on many campuses began with a top-down approach. "The source of the 'need' to assess—gubernatorial statements, accreditation requirements—imparts an aura of inauthenticity to the whole thing" (Marchese 1994, p. 7). With regard to the current status of assessment, the origin of outcomes assessment in stipulations from outsiders interested in accountability makes outcomes assessment seem external to the institution (Gandolfo 1995). In implementing assessment at West Virginia University and examining the literature about it:

. . . it became apparent that the process could be limited to data collection for purposes of accountability, and the faculty task force members balked at the thought of investing any energy in the process unless it would lead to improvement in . . . teaching and learning . . . (Gandolfo 1995, p. 6).

The AAUP's report on assessment takes criticism of the top-down imposition of assessment a step farther, questioning,

. . . the extent to which, despite disclaimers by its proponents, the mandatory assessment movement thus far has tended to represent a form of external state intrusion, bypassing the traditional roles of governing board, administration, and faculty, as well as both duplicating and diminishing the role of the independent regional accrediting bodies (American Association 1991, p. 51).

Faculty will resist any hint of external intrusion, and for many, assessment has given plenty of indication of an interest in such intrusion. At several major research universities, the direct involvement of the state converted lukewarm acceptance of internal assessment into vocal opposition to any kind of evaluation as a violation of institutional autonomy or academic freedom (Zguta 1989). As noted, states' future interest in accountability, rather than subsiding, may come to focus more on the content of what is being taught in colleges and universities (Ewell 1997). Faculty cannot be expected to ally themselves with movement in this direction. "Accountability as currently conceived cannot win widespread faculty support because it usurps our professional responsibility to decide what and how to teach and evaluate" (Peters 1994, p. 22).

Early state-mandated approaches to assessment focused primarily on the acquisition of basic skills (Ewell and Lisensky 1988). Faculty took little interest in proving that they were effective at transmitting skills that they associated with the award of a high school diploma. Further, this focus served to solidify the faculty's view that legislators and other external constituencies neither appreciated nor understood the proper role of colleges and universities in helping students to develop higher-order intellectual abilities.

On many campuses, assessment initially made its appearance as a stand-alone activity, with little consideration of

At several major research universities, the direct involvement of the state converted lukewarm acceptance of internal assessment into vocal opposition to any kind of evaluation as a violation of institutional autonomy or academic freedom.

potential links to teaching and learning, faculty development, or institutional research. Nor was thought given to linking assessment to institutional mission or goals. No ready constituency existed among the faculty to support these new enterprises, and faculty could identify few reasons to associate themselves with this new box on the organizational chart. Although many of these assessment operations were quite effective in data collection, they were less successful in linking these data to improvement of the curriculum. Most faculty saw little relationship between their day-to-day involvement with students and the operations of an assessment office.

At many higher education institutions, assessment became yet another addition to the already long list of faculty's service burdens. Assessment became another separate focus of committee work, tied not at all, or only incidentally, to teaching and learning or research. Faculty initially went about the business of planning for assessment with little contextual understanding of what motivated it and, in some disciplines, with few of the methodological skills essential to carrying it out. Faculty were assigned rather indiscriminately to the assessment committee rather than the parking committee or the student grievance committee, with little attention to questions of requisite knowledge or perspectives to appropriately engage the tasks at hand. Despite important recent attempts to elevate the importance of service in the overall expectations of faculty (Lynton 1994), service remains the least valued and least clearly defined role of faculty and the component with the least clearly associated historical traditions.

Assessment is about making decisions about effectiveness based on evidence, but proponents of assessment on many campuses have been slow to embody this commitment in their strategies for institutionalization. Advocates have been heavy on rhetoric and exhortation and light on evidence. A study of assessment programs at the 15 four-year public institutions in Virginia notes:

> The most surprising finding of this study was the absolute paucity of data reported. After seven years of assessment and three cycles of assessment reports, almost all institutions were still very reluctant to present data; rather, they reported generalities about data (E. Smith 1996, p. 5).

Skeptics on virtually every campus will ask for examples of how assessment has made a difference. They will ask for success stories from like institutions. Despite the presence of assessment programs on campuses throughout the country, it is difficult, if one moves beyond the list of five or six campuses that are mentioned repeatedly in the assessment literature, to cite compelling examples of assessment that have resulted in significant institutional change.

> *Having assembled 165 case studies based on some of the best assessment taking place at campuses across the country, I must say that the number of these cases containing concrete evidence that student performance has improved as a result of assessment is very small* (Banta et al. 1996, p. 343).

Similarly, institutional leaders have been slow to exemplify the transformative potential of assessment in their dealings with their own faculties. A dean, provost, or president can advance an institution's involvement in assessment much more dramatically by demonstrating that his or her own decision making about the allocation of resources has been influenced by carefully collected and interpreted data than by arguing eloquently and repeatedly how good it would be for the faculty to engage in assessment.

In many states and on many campuses, assessment appeared as another of those very unpopular "unfunded mandates." It is thus not surprising that campuses did not enthusiastically embrace the new "opportunities" presented by assessment. They were potentially costly add-ons, and nothing was taken away from an already full institutional agenda to make room for these new expectations. Interestingly, institutions repeated this same dysfunctional pattern in their allocation of these new responsibilities among faculty. While administrators on many campuses highlighted the importance of involvement in assessment, the institutional reward system reflected no new priorities.

> *Faculty know that what is valued is rewarded. Right now, with traditional incentive structures and behavior patterns set on so many of our campuses—despite the rhetoric about the "scholarship of representation"—we*

should not be surprised that faculty have not shifted
their priorities to include assessment (Ferren 1993, p. 2).

If faculty can see no benefit to being involved in assessment, then they are unlikely to be moved to participate. Few campuses have revised reward structures to recognize involvement in assessment.

If assessment is to be meaningful, it must be embedded in an institutional context that rewards taking risks. Yet assessment appeared on most campuses in times of budgetary cutbacks and associated faculty caution and defensiveness. Faculty need to be able to ask questions of importance to them about the curriculum and instruction without fearing that disclosing weaknesses will have negative repercussions. If assessment is to relate to improvement, it is important to know where improvement is needed. The culture in most institutions of higher education, however, has actively discouraged this kind of open questioning of effectiveness. For assessment to be useful and effective, faculty need to be empowered to ask difficult questions, and they need to be assured that if they receive unflattering answers to these questions, it will not be held against them. On many campuses in new assessment programs, no question has been asked to which faculty could not be sure that they already knew the answer and knew further that this answer would reflect positively on their current work.

> *Assessment must be designed and implemented within*
> *an atmosphere of trust, respect for individual differ-*
> *ences, and freedom to experiment and learn from fail-*
> *ures. Assessment must be viewed as self-correcting*
> *rather than as a stamp of approval or disapproval. In*
> *short, to assess is more than to judge; it is to build*
> (Braskamp 1991, p. 424).

Significant Inroads

> *One of the keys to success is to recognize and build on*
> *past and existing accomplishments and activities of*
> *faculty related to assessment of student academic*
> *achievement at whatever level [they] may be occurring*
> (Eisenman 1991, p. 462).

On campuses where existing assessment activities have been identified, highlighted, and given additional support, the faculty has more readily accepted assessment. Small grant programs at many institutions have provided the important boost to assessment projects that had already taken root within the faculty.

> Assessment programs that do not emerge from the unique needs of the institution and the specific capabilities of the faculty who are to carry them out and respond to the findings run into significant resistance. . . . To get commitment, faculty must be involved at the outset, and faculty must be prepared for the same kind of frustration, division, and negotiation while hammering out an assessment plan that their colleagues experienced in shaping the curriculum (Ferren 1993, p. 5).

Moreover, the goals of assessment should be connected to the momentum evident in curricular reform, faculty development, and program review (Ferren 1993). Faculty more readily embrace assessment when it is seen as a means, not an end. For example, when support for new program development has been linked to evidence provided, faculty have been eager to seek consultation about how to gather evidence on effectiveness. Similarly, when a departmental or programmatic need is identified through assessment, for example, a need for the addition of a certain specialty not available among the current faculty, and when the process provides support for hiring a new person or providing other new resources, faculty may be easily persuaded of the value of assessment.

Classroom assessment has taken root on many campuses independent of a broader campus assessment agenda and has traveled a separate track, often linked to campus teaching and learning centers or other faculty development initiatives—and often not formally labeled "assessment." Providing recognition and additional support to such activities by encouraging a breadth of perspectives on assessment and discouraging ideological purity ensures greater acceptance among the faculty.

Classroom assessment has taken root on many campuses independent of a broader campus assessment agenda and has traveled a separate track, often linked to campus teaching and learning centers or other faculty development initiatives—and often not formally labeled "assessment."

> While faculty-to-faculty initiatives may lack something in polish and seem "homegrown" in many ways, what

is lost in expertise is made up for in collegiality and confidence. Many of the most engaging and effective assessment efforts, such as the Harvard Assessment Seminars, have this same "homegrown" quality (Ferren 1993, p. 6).

Faculty are much more accepting of assessment in general when they are able to identify specific practices or projects of their liking included under a broad umbrella of assessment activities on campus.

THE FACULTY'S INVOLVEMENT IN ASSESSMENT: Examples from the Campuses

This section identifies six models for implementing assessment on campus: (1) assessment as part of an institution's fabric; (2) assessment as related to accountability; (3) assessment as an administrative service; (4) assessment as scholarship; (5) assessment as an opportunity for teaching; and (6) assessment as an add-on responsibility. It also identifies campuses where assessment falls into one of these categories, and discusses assessment in terms of the role faculty play.

The faculty's involvement in assessment spans a broad spectrum of activities and degrees of engagement. Institutional philosophy of assessment will dictate the extent and kind of involvement by faculty. At some institutions, faculty own the assessment process from beginning to end—developing policy, creating questions about and approaches to assessment, collecting data and analyzing them, and using interpretations of the results to improve the curriculum. At other institutions, faculty are involved in only one or two aspects of assessment, perhaps developing policy or using results, with the majority of data collection and analysis carried out by an assessment or institutional research office. At some institutions, assessment is embedded in the faculty's daily teaching activities. At still others, assessment is external to the curriculum and instruction and may fall under the categories of faculty service or scholarship. And at yet other institutions, faculty are not involved at all in assessment.

In large part, administrative leadership will determine the way faculty will come to view their role in assessment. A review of over 162 case studies of assessment concludes:

> *It is quite clear from the case studies . . . that effective administrative and faculty leadership is an essential condition if assessment is to succeed on campus. Effective leadership . . . is a means to offset some of the institutional barriers to change. These barriers include (1) complexity of assessment; (2) professional sensitivity toward assessment (that is, the view that assessment is a threat to academic freedom and the appropriate exercise of faculty judgment); (3) political sensitivity toward assessment; and (4) the time necessary to implement assessment efforts* (Banta et al. 1996, p. 63).

One consequence of this major role of administrative leadership is that when senior administrators change, the campus's approach to assessment is also likely to change. Many institutions have started with one vision of assessment, which altered abruptly when senior administrators changed or, in a few cases, when the state's leadership changed. Such abrupt changes fire faculty cynicism about "the agenda of the week."

The way administrators choose to present assessment to a campus will determine to a great extent how the campus perceives the issue. In a few cases, a faculty entrepreneur will fill the void when a leader is needed and will begin shaping the institution's response to the issue. Much early work in assessment was done by individual faculty entrepreneurs who either got excited about the possibility for improving students' educational experiences or were curious about the kind of impact the institution was having on students' cognitive, personal, and social development.

If assessment has been a significant part of the fabric of the institution for a sufficient time, then the campus's approach to assessment may determine the choice of leadership or at least influence a new leader to continue in a particular direction. If an administrator frames the discussion of assessment in a particular light, it will shape both the faculty's and students' responses. Assessment can be presented as an effort essential to scholarly reflection on a campus's collective educational endeavors, providing information that will allow the quality of educational offerings to be improved, or it can be presented as a burden that the campus must endure to satisfy others.

Each institutional approach to assessment noted earlier demands a different kind of involvement from the faculty, ranging from integral agent, to passive consumer, to noninvolved bystander. The rest of this section presents samples of institutional approaches to assessment, with illustrations of the role that faculty play.

Assessment as Part of an Institution's Fabric
"There is no question that assessment as an integral part of the students' learning process and as a means of evaluating programs and the institution will endure at Alverno" (Loacker and Mentkowski 1993, p. 20). Before the NIE report (Study Group 1984), state mandates, and the AAHE Assessment Forum, there was Alverno College with a curriculum developed under the leadership of Sister Joel Reid during the late 1960s and early

1970s. At Alverno, the achievement of specific educational competencies drives the curriculum and assessment.

With clear and measurable goals, assessment of individual students and the curriculum became manageable tasks (Alverno College Faculty 1985; Loacker 1988; Mentkowski and Loacker 1985). Strong links between assessment and the curriculum ensured that improvement of the curriculum would be a continuous process. Faculty were able to see the impact of their teaching strategies through the evaluation of students' performance by others and by themselves.

> *The basic responsibility for articulating our assessment principles and practice and constantly refining the process by which they inform each other lies with the group of representative faculty members who make up the Assessment Council. They direct the development of collegewide instruments and criteria that assess abilities across the disciplines* (Loacker and Mentkowski 1993, p. 10).

The faculty's role in assessment is key to Alverno's teaching mission. The traditional grading system was replaced by the requirement that all graduates be able to demonstrate mastery of all of the designated competencies. Assessment replaced evaluation (grading) as the way in which faculty provided feedback to students on their progress and certified to the public that they deserved college degrees.

Though no other institution of higher education has more thoroughly embraced assessment than Alverno, at other colleges, mostly other early pioneers in assessment like King's College and Kean College of New Jersey (Paskow 1988), educational missions are intertwined closely with an understanding of the importance of comprehensive assessment. Faculty in these institutions have come to view assessment as an essential tool for providing information that will help them become more effective teachers.

In the 1970s, under the leadership of Charles McClain and Darrell Krueger, Northeast Missouri State University (renamed Truman State University in 1996) used assessment to examine the quality of the educational experiences being provided to students. McClain and Krueger challenged the faculty to demonstrate that they were making a difference in the lives of students. The institution used a variety of assessment strategies, initially adopting a value-added model to demonstrate the impact the institution was having on students' intellectual development. The language, as well as the tools, of assessment became part of the faculty's consciousness. Faculty were encouraged to adopt a self-reflective mode, and improving the undergraduate experience at Northeast Missouri/Truman State came to be viewed as a collective responsibility. Faculty at Northeast Missouri/Truman State are actively involved in the generation and use of assessment information at both the departmental and institutional level. Students also have come to play a part in assessment, not only as providers of information, but also as shapers of the approaches being used. Indeed, one student/alumnus has published several articles and presented papers at conferences on assessment (Bambenek 1996). The value of assessment definitely has permeated the institution.

> *Without a doubt, the assessment culture at Northeast Missouri causes the campus community to think more clearly about the desired outcomes of a college degree and as a result to analyze which methods, processes, and curricula are most likely to achieve the desired results. . . . The future of assessment depends on the university leadership's continued emphasis on high academic standards and continuous improvement, frequent use of assessment information, and creation of vehicles for faculty-administrative conversations grounded in data* (Young and Knight 1993, pp. 31–32).

Indeed, the identity of Northeast Missouri/Truman State is now so closely tied to its work in assessment that an advertisement in *Chronicle of Higher Education* (July 3, 1997, p. B46) for a new vice president for academic affairs stated, "Truman is nationally recognized for its innovative assessment program and its commitment to excellence in teaching and learning." The advertisement goes on to describe the successful candidate for the position as a person who has "a strong, demonstrable commitment to the liberal arts and sciences as well as to the proactive use of assessment data for the improvement of teaching and learning."

At Alverno, Northeast Missouri/Truman State, King's College, and Kean College, the president and other administrative leaders engaged the faculty in discussions of ways to improve students' educational experiences. Assessment was

presented to the faculty as a tool to use in better document-
ing the impact the institution was having and to provide
data as a basis for decision making.

> *One of the most important benefits of assessment is the
> data's ability to raise the critical questions, thereby set-
> ting the institutional discussion and decision agenda.
> The data can assist an institution in identifying problem
> areas and in monitoring programmatic change. How-
> ever, faculty-administrative conversations, grounded in
> the data, provide the primary opportunities for univer-
> sity leadership to effect positive change* (Young and
> Knight 1993, p. 29).

These examples suggest the importance of the interplay
between administrative leadership and the faculty's participation in developing a "culture of evidence," where assessment is taken seriously in the institution's day-to-day decision making.

Assessment as Related to Accountability

Several different approaches to using assessment as an institutional response to concerns about accountability have been
attempted. With few exceptions, faculty have played only a
minor role or no role in developing such policies. Frequently,
however, these mandates have caused faculty to scramble to
undo or to minimize the potential damage when programs
were being developed by policy makers with little understanding of either assessment or higher education.

For example, the state of Florida in 1982 adopted a "rising
junior exam" (the College-Level Academic Skills Test or
CLAST) and mandated it for all students as a means of ensuring accountability in relation to the quality of undergraduate programs. Because the exam was aimed at establishing
minimal competency, this program most directly affected the
Florida community college system—the open-admissions
part of the higher education system in Florida. With regard
to the faculty's role in responding to this mandate:

> *Presenting the faculty viewpoint of entry/exit testing is a
> challenging task because each member, even within a
> single institution, has been affected in a different way.
> Some faculty who teach senior and graduate-level*

*courses at large universities have not been affected by
these changes, but faculty who teach freshmen and
sophomores, whether at four-year schools or at community colleges, have had incredible demands placed on
them. Even in community colleges, some faculty members' workload has increased tremendously, while others
have not been affected much* (Ciereszko 1987, p. 67).

Shifts in course assignments and class sizes have resulted
from a need to ensure that sufficiently small sections of
courses were available in areas related to CLAST's areas of
emphasis. This situation caused enrollment in non-CLAST-
related classes to swell, because more faculty resources were
being devoted to CLAST preparatory classes. While faculty
have responded through institutional pressure, it has not
been without cost. And questions remain about whether this
approach has made a difference in the overall quality of
students' educational experiences.

In 1981, Tennessee became one of the first states to adopt
a performance-funding model. This initiative thrust Tennessee institutions—most notably the University of Tennessee–
Knoxville, whose response to performance funding was led
by Trudy Banta—very quickly into the forefront of the assessment movement. Unlike Florida, where a particular test
at a specific point in a student's program of study was mandated, Tennessee did not specify particular tests, but rather
required a number of areas to be assessed: evidence of a
program's accreditation; evaluation of instruction through
validated tests or peer review; measures of general education
outcomes; evaluation of institutional programs and services by
students, alumni, and employers; and evaluation planning for
renewal and improvement. Points were awarded in each of
the categories and used to determine the level of additional
performance-based funding the institution would receive, up
to a 5 percent financial supplement.

*Perhaps the most important lessons learned from Tennes-
see's attempt to budget on the basis of instructional effectiveness have to do with the planning process. Being pa-
tient and persistent, having the broad-based involvement
of institutional faculty and administrators, and linking
assessment strategies to daily teaching/learning activities
are all key elements* (Levy 1986, p. 26).

A review of state policy regarding the accountability of higher education notes:

Faculty involvement in and support of all aspects of the [assessment] program are essential components of success. . . . Performance-based funding should be derived from additional resources. . . . If a performance incentive is used, the funds should supplement those generated through the usual funding formulas and should be limited to a relatively small proportion of each campus's general operating budget (Halpern 1987, p. 110).

The Ohio State Program Excellence competitions provided a model for such an approach. Faculty-controlled assessment that documented high-quality programs resulted in supplemental funds.

Institutions in Ohio were invited to select departments that they believed were providing a high-quality undergraduate education and to forward proposals for supplemental funding (awards ranged from $100,000 to $200,000). These proposals were to provide "evidence" to support the claim of excellence. The proposals were read by external reviewers, who visited the campuses and submitted evaluation reports, and final awards were determined by a panel that reviewed both the proposals and the evaluators' reports.

In the first round of competition, many of the awards went to two-year institutions, with the state's four-year institutions proportionally underrepresented. The two-year institutions clearly were prepared to make a stronger case for the excellence of their work. Thus, four-year universities were motivated to begin active assessment programs to document the quality of their efforts. Faculty members played a central role in collecting the evidence of quality, as the awards were made at the departmental level (Tafel and Schilling 1992).

Assessment as an Administrative Service
Some institutions have opened assessment offices that serve as a resource for faculty in identifying questions about assessment and developing or selecting appropriate instruments to answer them. At its best, this model can provide faculty who feel they are not trained in assessment with support in getting started and consultation on collecting data and interpreting results. Indeed, the initial products from this

approach are often more sophisticated than results produced by faculty "amateurs."

If, however, assessment is viewed as an integral part of the scholar/teacher role, then it is important that faculty have a feel for the data. Just as faculty probably would not feel comfortable writing articles based on someone else's summary of the relevant data because they would not have an experiential understanding of the work and thus its strengths and weaknesses, so it is with their response to information about assessment. To understand and interpret data—to get behind "outcomes"—to the extent that they make a difference in daily practice, it is important that faculty understand the instruments used and the way the results are assembled.

Having an assessment office may initially seem very attractive to faculty, because it gets them off the hook. With such an office on campus, however, faculty may become more likely to view assessment as the responsibility of that office. They see it as the job of this office to "do" assessment, leaving faculty free to carp about and critique both the process and the results. Faculty in this situation become, at best, more passive consumers of information provided by the assessment office, rather than shapers and owners of such information, and, at worst, totally uninformed about and/or distrustful of assessment.

At Ball State University, however, the Office of Assessment seems to have been reasonably successful in avoiding many of these pitfalls. The office consults extensively with departments and individual faculty wishing to become involved in assessment. It assists in the process from beginning to end but leaves the faculty to make the key decisions. It manages a pool of money to support faculty in undertaking assessment. These funds are distributed competitively, and a faculty committee with representatives from each college decides which projects will be funded (Palomba and Moore 1996).

James Madison University, Virginia Military Institute, and the University of Maryland all offer interesting variations of this approach. Assessment offices at those campuses have been able to develop extensive programs that have had an impact on their campuses and on the faculty working there.

Many community colleges have used an office of institutional research to spearhead assessment; a particularly notable one is the office at Johnson City Community College.

Many community colleges have used an office of institutional research to spearhead assessment; a particularly notable one is the office at Johnson City Community College.

Among other projects, this office has examined the success of remedial courses in preparing students to be successful in their nonremedial work. The results of this study, when shared with the Underprepared Students Committee comprising faculty and staff, led to recommended specific steps to improve the situation (for example, mandatory counseling for underprepared students). This proposal was then adopted by the administration (Seybert and Soltz 1996).

Assessment as Scholarship
Some institutions have come to understand assessment as drawing upon skills that are integral to scholarship: using one's intellectual curiosity to frame questions and to develop strategies for answering those questions, to collect information related to the questions, to evaluate the implications of these data, to apply the new information, and to reframe the question and begin the process anew. In this approach, assessment is scholarly activity. Boyer's notion of the "scholarship of application" applies here. Individual faculty or groups of faculty carry out the assessment from beginning to end, viewing it in a way similar to any other scholarly activity. While in this model assessment may not be as integrated into the fabric of the institution, it may play an important role in the professional lives of individual faculty. These entrepreneurs are able to provide the institution with valuable information about its impact on students. Many institutions, when they begin the process of assessment, find that they have several faculty members who have already been carrying out small assessment projects. Building upon these efforts can be a wise strategy for assuring that assessment is institutionalized.

Miami University's assessment program began with questions about the relative effectiveness of two common models of general education—distribution versus core curricula. With support from FIPSE, the researcher used the concurrent existence of these two curricular models on Miami's campus as an opportunity to bring evidence to national conversations about the best curricular designs for undergraduate education. Strategies found most effective in this study were further refined in the portfolio-based assessment undertaken with the implementation of a new liberal education curriculum at Miami in 1990 (Schilling and Schilling 1993a, 1993b) and became central to the development of yet another FIPSE-supported project on increasing expectations for students' academic effort.

At SUNY–Fredonia, a former dean for liberal and continuing education brought together a group of faculty to design and carry out assessment in relation to implementation of the new liberal education program. The faculty created a number of imaginative approaches to assessment that were specifically tied to the goals of the new liberal education program.

> *Since our General College Program (GCP) focuses on broadly defined intellectual skills to be developed through any of a variety of courses, we also thought that our findings would have little impact on our colleagues unless we could show that whatever improvement we found was attributable to our particular GCP, rather than to a generic college experience. . . . We were under no mandate to prove ourselves to any external public* (Amiran, Schilling, and Schilling 1993, p. 72).

As a result of using faculty-developed measures specifically tied to the specific goals of the program, faculty at Fredonia were quickly able to make recommendations to the entire faculty about the implications of the results of their assessment. Because they were taking a scholarly approach, they were also able to express a number of sophisticated cautions about the use of the results, noting problems such as the difficulty in initiating changes during a time of budget constraints, ignorance of basic understandings of adult development in relation to complex skills, and the resulting puzzle:

> *We know perfectly well that most of our freshmen are generally different from our upperclassmen in their academic abilities (teaching a freshman general education class is obviously quite different from teaching a class of juniors and seniors) [so] why are we (and most other researchers) not able to demonstrate more dramatic changes than any that appeared in our measurements?* (Amiran, Schilling, and Schilling 1993, p. 77).

The work at Fredonia demonstrates the amount of learning that can take place when faculty engage assessment as an intellectual activity. According to the director of the Harvard Assessment Seminars:

Anyone who teaches at Harvard for any length of time gets caught up in a continuing debate. In my 25 years here, I certainly have. The debate centers on how faculty members can help students learn as effectively as possible. My colleagues think long and hard about the best ways to advise students, or to teach classes, or even to teach outside of a classroom. Doing these many parts of our job well is a widely shared goal. And translating good intentions into practices poses a continuing challenge (Light 1992, p. 4).

Funds provided by the president's office helped bring together a number of key faculty leaders over dinner to talk about questions that they had about students' experiences and the curriculum at Harvard. These faculty played a key role in identifying the questions that would be of greatest interest to them and the answers that would cause them to change their classroom behaviors.

From these conversations, a number of projects emerged that have been reported to the campus and widely distributed throughout the higher education community thus far in two monographs (Light 1990, 1992) and numerous conference presentations. These publications have had a substantial impact on higher education nationally, not only because they pursued some very interesting questions, but also because campus leaders could point to the fact that "even Harvard" was engaged in assessment of student outcomes. Not surprisingly, assessment was conducted in a scholarly manner:

At the outset we decided that to learn what works best for students we should gather in-depth data directly from those students. So we did. Of the 570 undergraduates participating in the effort, many were interviewed several times. Some were interviewed extensively by faculty members. Others spoke at length to fellow students. . . . These conversations have yielded some detailed and remarkably personal data about students' experience at college (Light 1992, p. 4).

At Northern Virginia Community College, faculty working with the coordinator of academic assessment have developed a general education assessment program focused on the disciplines that contribute to the program. Each department develops an approach that is appropriate to its discipline. Widely ranging approaches, from common final exams, students' projects, and assignments to portfolios and videotapes, have been used.

> *The assessment process provided opportunities for professional development. To develop their expertise, faculty were given the results of an ERIC search for assessment measures in their discipline. Some faculty on the committees presented papers about their findings at state, regional, and national conferences* (Robertson and Simpson 1996, p. 193).

Indeed, many campuses have discovered that assessment can be a way to reengage faculty who have not recently been active in scholarship in national conversations about assessment as well as to contribute to the literature on pedagogy in their disciplines.

Assessment as an Opportunity for Teaching
A few institutions, primarily smaller liberal arts colleges (most notably Hope College and Union College), have been able to transform assessment from an institutional burden to an exciting opportunity for teaching. Because many institutions do not have the resources to provide release time for faculty to conduct assessment projects, let alone to create an assessment office, assessment has been seen as a competitor for scarce human resources, distracting the faculty's attention from their central role as teachers.

At least two institutions, however, have realized the desirability of merging these two functions by using students to conduct the assessment from beginning to end. These institutions have been able to develop imaginative approaches to assessment by putting students in seminars where they are asked to read relevant literature, formulate questions, design an approach, identify or create appropriate measures, explore ethical issues in assessment, collect data, analyze and interpret this information, and make recommendations about the implications of their findings. Students seem able to ask very interesting questions and to know how to get their classmates to cooperate, to take assessment seriously, and to provide information that will be useful and authentic. At the end of the class, students have had the opportunity to present their assessment projects to the campus, often in presentations to campus groups or through written reports.

While some might question the legitimacy of providing credit for such courses, others have argued that assessment will be an important skill for all college graduates to have, regardless of the profession they enter. Thus, assessment as practiced in these institutions has provided a rare opportunity to kill two birds with one stone—to provide an important educational experience for students while also providing the institution with valuable information about the impact it is having on its students.

Assessment as an Add-on Responsibility

One of the most common ways assessment is handled on campuses is for an administrator to assign a committee and/ or an individual the task as part of their service responsibilities, frequently providing no leadership on the issue and providing few financial resources for carrying it out. Often the office of institutional research is charged with carrying out assessment with little recognition of the implications of this decision. Administrators, in these cases, fail to recognize the potential of assessment and, like many faculty members, just want to get it out of the way. They miss the opportunity to shift the campus culture to one that values evidence in decision making.

We are committed to weaving assessment into every aspect of CGA [the Coast Guard Academy]. It is only with a truly integrated comprehensive assessment plan that we can know our strength, identify our weaknesses, and pursue our quest for excellence (Stevens and Haas 1996, p. 5).

From these examples, it is clear that for assessment to make a difference on campus, faculty must come to see it as part of their responsibilities as professionals. If assessment is to move from a "minimal effort–minimal impact" mode, faculty must develop the understanding that assessment is not a foreign, hostile intrusion into academic life, but is rather a quintessentially scholarly activity. Assessment calls upon faculty to bring all of their professional skills and creativity to bear on how best to understand the impact their work has on students and how to increase the positive impact on students' intellectual and personal development.

If assessment is to move from a "minimal effort–minimal impact" mode, faculty must develop the understanding that assessment is not a foreign, hostile intrusion into academic life, but is rather a quintessentially scholarly activity.

In the end, our goal at Harvard is to work steadily to enhance student learning, to encourage and assess innovations in the classroom, and ultimately to enrich each student's full experience here as much as possible. I know that despite the extraordinary diversity among American colleges, nearly all share these three goals (Light 1992, p. 7).

ENVISIONING ASSESSMENT AS A FACULTY ROLE

This section begins by listing six conditions that are necessary for faculty to identify assessment as an integral part of their role and concludes by offering a set of principles for developing effective assessment programs that will engage faculty in meaningful assessment.

Based on a rather traditional notion of the academy that identifies faculty as the heart of the institution and the primary agents behind any significant institutional change, each preceding section argues that the impact of assessment on higher education is likely to be minimal if faculty do not more thoroughly embrace the enterprise. The preceding sections illuminate sources of faculty resistance to assessment and identify changes that have occurred in assessment over time that could result in the faculty's greater acceptance of assessment. They also note, however, that faculty do not respond well to external mandates for change. What, then, might motivate faculty to greater involvement and investment in assessment? We believe that faculty will identify assessment as consistent with their role when six conditions are satisfied:

1. Assessment must be embedded in a fiscal and policy context that supports innovation under administrative leadership that provides vision and support.
2. Assessment must be grounded in significant questions that faculty find interesting.
3. Assessment must rely on evidence and forms of judgment that disciplinary specialists find credible.
4. Assessment must be rooted in a language and metaphors appropriate to the context.
5. Assessment must be identified as a stimulus to reflective practice.
6. Assessment must accommodate the nature of faculty life in the academy.

A Supportive Fiscal and Policy Context
When assessment is linked strategically with other important processes related to improvement, such as planning and program review, many objections from the faculty vanish. Again, most faculty find no interest in assessment for its own sake, but many can be persuaded of the potential contributions of systematic data collection and analysis to ongoing improvement of teaching and learning. Acceptance is most likely on campuses that reward risk taking by faculty. Administrators

who provide a vision for the institution that goes well beyond the short term can do much to encourage risk taking. Then assessment can play an important role in supporting innovation. For true innovation to occur, however, faculty must be assured that they can ask difficult questions about teaching and the curriculum. A cardinal rule guiding most current assessment programs is "don't ask any questions for which you cannot afford to know the answer." But it is these very questions that are being avoided—how much difference are we making? how could we do a better job with our students?—that colleges and universities must begin to address if they are to significantly improve students' learning. Sustaining excellent programs requires much more than bean counting. When faculty are encouraged to ask fundamental questions about students' learning in the interest of offering the most effective educational programs, assessment can play a key role in providing answers.

When assessment feeds naturally into ongoing institutional planning or ongoing cycles of peer review, faculty can see a clear stake in their involvement and the obvious incentives for their participation. Faculty historically have assiduously defended their right to exercise control over decision making in areas related to curriculum and instruction. Assessment can be a central element in this decision making, moving beyond reliance on assertions of faith or familiar anecdotes.

Questions of Interest to the Faculty
There is little doubt that questions about the effectiveness of teaching and learning will loom large on the horizon for most faculty as we move into the 21st century. At no time in the history of higher education have faculty faced concurrently so many different challenges to business as usual as they do today. The landscape is changing rapidly around the faculty. They are faced with more choices about their work with students than ever before, and they likely will welcome assistance in making these choices. Among the many challenges faculty face are:

• *The increased diversity of students.* Pressures for access and equitable treatment have resulted in increased diversity at most colleges and universities. And we have only begun to realize the impact on curriculum and instruction of admitting more diverse populations. As they face challenges to content and modes of instruction based on questions of their relative adequacy for different groups of students, faculty will need more evidence about the effectiveness of various strategies for the students they serve. Indeed, assessment can help make visible for faculty the differences between their own experiences as learners in the classroom and current students' approaches to learning. Assessment can aid faculty in sustaining the excellence of instruction in the face of very different student populations.

- *A broader range of pedagogical strategies.* A focus on learners and learning provokes consideration of the effectiveness of various modes of instruction. On virtually every campus today, faculty development initiatives are offered to expose faculty to a broader range of pedagogical options. But how are faculty to decide how much they will emphasize lectures, discussions, discovery-based approaches, collaborative learning groups, or service learning? As knowledge about a greater range of pedagogical alternatives becomes available to faculty, choices for course design will become much more complex. Carefully conducted studies of the effectiveness of various pedagogical strategies for achieving varied goals in diverse contexts could guide the faculty's choices about the design of courses and curricula.

- *The availability of new technologies.* Will students' unlimited access to information through new technologies alter the relationship between faculty and students? Can students learn some kinds of materials more effectively through discovery-oriented, self-directed study on a computer than through traditional classroom instruction? How effective are computer technologies in various forms of instruction? Is distance learning an effective substitute for traditional classroom instruction? As faculty have greater access to technology for use in instruction, information on the effectiveness of these new modes will be essential to guide decision making about their proper uses.

- *Pressures to credit prior experience and to facilitate articulation and transfer.* How are faculty to determine the worth of their coursework in a broader academic marketplace? How are they to determine whether a student's prior preparation at another institution provides needed preparation for entering advanced courses or whether experience in the workforce has ensured needed competencies to complete more advanced work? As realities conspire to limit further the number of students who complete their undergraduate experience in four to five years at one institution, better modes of assessment will need to be developed to facilitate articulation and transfer. The aggressiveness of proprietary institutions and corporate colleges, and the large and well-funded training components of many corporations in seeking evidence to document the effectiveness of their programs in delivering on promises to students could also motivate faculty in more traditional colleges and universities to seek better evidence of the effectiveness of their programs to continue their edge in the competition for students.

Faculty will seek answers to these and many more questions about their effectiveness. Assessment that begins with the questions of the faculty and helps provide answers to the questions faculty care about offers significant potential for institutional transformation. Assessment can play an important role in making the curriculum visible to faculty. By focusing together on the work of students, faculty can begin to develop collective interests. Fiercely autonomous faculty may begin, in reflecting with colleagues on the results of assessment, to make the important transition from talking about "my" students to talking about "our" students. Assessment can facilitate conversations about collective dreams and common goals.

Reams and reams of existing reports should inform decisions about curriculum and instruction, but they have not and never will because they are not related to the day-to-day concerns of faculty about their subject matter and their students. Assessment that will have an impact must begin and end with the faculty. Adding fuel to the existing fire by beginning with the faculty's questions will likely have more positive results than trying to ignite a new flicker under some question dreamed up by an administrator or staff person.

Credible Evidence and Forms of Judgment
Providing a more adequate conceptual and methodological framework for assessment will assure greater acceptance among the faculty. Simplistic or reductionist approaches that do not capture the diversity and complexity of perspectives in the academy are unlikely to win the faculty's acceptance. Approaches to assessment that rely on multiple methods be-

gin to capture this complexity. They also can serve as an impetus to conversations that cut across disciplinary lines. Cherished traditions of peer review in higher education have their origins in a deep respect for expertise. Judgments of specialists are accorded particular status. Assessment strategies that rely on these judgments of specialists in proclaiming excellence are quite consistent with the faculty's role expectations.

Appropriate Language and Metaphors

It is tempting in the face of so many new challenges confronting faculty to call for a radical transformation of the faculty's role, to argue that faculty have not been prepared to deal with these new challenges and that the academy must be dramatically reshaped. Early calls for the faculty's involvement in assessment bore this mark. Rather than linking assessment with traditional faculty roles, assessment was presented as a new activity demanding the faculty's time and attention. Not surprisingly, the number of new recruits drawn to the ranks was small. Richard Light's work at Harvard is an alternative to this approach (1990, 1992). Light was successful in identifying assessment with naturally occurring conversations about teaching and learning. He planted no new seeds. Rather, he cultivated and nurtured the germs of ideas already alive in the minds and conversations of faculty. Moreover:

Assessment efforts have been further hampered by specialized language that has made outsiders of faculty trained in traditional disciplines who are turned off by terms such as "performance criteria" and "construct validity" (Ferren 1993, p. 3).

On many campuses, significant progress has been made on the assessment agenda only after a very purposeful commitment has been made by all involved to avoid the "A word." Like many new movements, assessment has developed its own language and mode of discourse. Specialized languages serve an important role in defining and reinforcing group membership and status for those who speak the language. But by defining insiders, we concurrently define outsiders. Much of the important work of assessment can be done without the mystification of new language and vocabulary that raises faculty's hackles. Although they may be deeply interested in the improvement of teaching and learning,

On many campuses, significant progress has been made on the assessment agenda only after a very purposeful commitment has been made by all involved to avoid the "A word."

---

most faculty simply do not have either the interest or the motivation to learn the new language of assessment.

To engage faculty in assessment, it is also important to capture the essential components of the process in metaphors that are congenial to life in the academy. The language of productivity associated with early accountability initiatives carried too many of the marks of business and industry to be easily accepted by most faculty. Here again, the focus on "conversation" appeals to many. Archeological or anthropological metaphors, for example, can be useful by introducing the idea of students' work as artifacts of the curriculum to be studied as keys to the values of institutional culture. Auditory metaphors—listening to the sounds of the curriculum—may capture the imagination of other faculty. (See Schilling and Schilling 1993a and 1993b for suggestions of other metaphors that capture essential features of assessment and invite broader participation.) It is important, however, to reflect on the likely associations of any metaphor before attempting to cultivate a receptive audience.

Assessment as a Stimulus to Reflective Practice

The assessment movement has been criticized for misdiagnosing the problem in higher education and distracting attention from effective solutions, being at best a way to diagnose, not cure, ills (Benjamin 1990). In attending to this criticism, however, it is important not to lose track of the value of diagnosis. Assessment can provide a set of strategies or procedures to use in identifying and clarifying problems. In this sense, assessment is a powerful stimulus to reflective practice. Because faculty are so fiercely autonomous, collective efforts to cure systemic ills will come about very, very slowly. But enough individual reflection on daily practice informed by assessment of activities—much of which is occurring already, whether labeled classroom assessment or not—could radically transform the character of instruction in colleges in universities. Using assessment as a stimulus to reflective practice is quite consistent with the faculty's role.

Accommodating Assessment to the Nature of Faculty

Successful assessment programs must be durable; they must be developed with an eye toward the long term. Beyond an Alverno College, however, it will be unusual to have a large number of faculty willing to make long-term, substantial commitments to involvement in assessment—which does not mean that faculty cannot play a significant role in a durable institutional assessment plan. It is not the case that the majority of faculty on a campus must identify the transformative potential of assessment for assessment to have a significant impact. Conversations among a relatively small group of faculty can offer sufficient impetus to spur institutional change. It is also the case that faculty members' commitments to assessment may be episodic and matched to their current interests and passions. Just as most faculty will assume an important role in a project to reform the curriculum or in editing a journal or in another similar significant professional activity for a relatively short term (say two to four years), a reasonable number of faculty would be willing to be involved in assessment if they understand that the responsibility for conducting assessment will, over time, rotate among their faculty colleagues. The size of this number and thus the available corps of faculty volunteers for involvement in assessment will increase proportionally to the perceived impact of assessment on campus practices. Faculty will see a role for themselves in assessment if the work has an observable institutional impact and if it can be accommodated within a typical faculty member's schedule. Overly ambitious assessment programs will lose the faculty's support.

Similarly, many necessary components of successful assessment programs will hold little interest for faculty. In fact, the faculty's interest in assessment will dissipate quickly if staff support is not provided for many of the tedious or technical portions of assessment. Faculty will involve themselves in those components of assessment that they see as consistent with a faculty role—and technician and research assistant are not among them.

Some Principles for Envisioning Assessment as a Role for Faculty

The availability of an almost unlimited range of methods unfortunately leaves many assessment programs far too consumed by methodology and not appropriately concerned about the utility of assessment practice in the broader institutional context. In trying to link ongoing data collection with the agenda for improving programs in colleges and universities, we have formulated a set of principles that we believe are embodied in some of the current best practices in assessment (Schilling and Schilling 1997). These principles are offered as suggestions for consideration in the development of any program of assessment that will significantly involve faculty.

1. In recognition of the enormity of the task, *good assessment proceeds by identifying manageable chunks.* The agenda for assessment might be thought of as working toward a CAT scan of our educational process—a three-dimensional picture composed by assembling thousands of slices taken at varying angles. Each slice adds a bit more clarity and acuity to our view of the overall process. We should not be daunted by the total number of slices we will need to make the definitive diagnosis. Instead, we should recognize that each slice contributes to our total understanding.

2. We need to commit ourselves to *an ongoing process.* Assessment is not something we get over; it is something we get on with.

3. We need to commit ourselves to *cumulative and incremental models of understanding,* recognizing that understanding the whole picture of any dynamic system will always be an elusive goal.

4. We need to abandon the fallacy of the perfect measure, recognize that *assessment will necessarily be imperfect,* and avoid the unproductive "paralysis of analysis."

5. We must model the processes that we would like rooted in our institutions. We must demonstrate the value of data in decision making by *making optimal use of existing data* before we collect new data. It is far easier to build momentum for assessment by recognizing data previously collected as a valid endeavor rather than by imposing some new definition and standard and trying to cultivate new efforts. Similarly, compelling demonstrations of the utility of data in decision making leave people far more inclined to commit to the collection of new data. We all know of far too many examples of data collected and never analyzed.

6. Meaningful assessment *raises as many questions as it answers.* Given the complexity of the curricular issues that are likely to be our focus, we are unlikely to reach definitive and unquestionable conclusions about effectiveness.

7. Assessment *is an interpretive enterprise,* involving judgment, not just measurement. Values permeate considerations of data on effectiveness.

8. Valid approaches to assessment recognize and accommodate the institution's *multiple perspectives*. Many faculty reject reductionist approaches to assessment that capture only one perspective or way of knowing or kind of evidence. Chemists and poets do not process information in the same way and do not reach the same conclusions, even when presented with identical evidence.
9. Assessment practices cannot be divorced from their context and institutional history. They are necessarily *tied to local culture*. Practices or evidence from one campus cannot be simply transported to another without translation that is sensitive to local meanings and traditions.

We tell our students that the unexamined life is not worth living. The institutional corollary of this statement may be that the unexamined college or university is not worth attending. Colleges and universities face many decisions and need good information to aid them in making the kinds of decisions that will improve learning for students. Much has changed in institutions of higher education over time—knowledge has exploded, fields have developed and branched and branched again. Ideas about teaching and learning have become much more complex. New kinds of institutions have developed, and new missions have been developed for others. Colleges and universities serve altogether new populations. New complex bureaucracies support the complexity of institutional structures that have evolved over time.

Amid all of these changes, though, a few things have remained constant. Although threatened from many directions, the traditional role of the faculty in developing and overseeing curriculum and instruction for the most part has not changed, nor for the most part has the primary role of the faculty in ensuring quality control. Quality assurance in these new complex organizations must take on a new seriousness and appropriate new complexity. Threats to faculty control will continue. Both internal and external constituencies may be harder to persuade, and better arguments and better forms of evidence will likely be necessary. But faculty will continue to play the major role in proclaiming and sustaining excellence in American colleges and universities. Their involvement in assessment will be key to their success in these tasks.

REFERENCES

The Educational Resources Information Center (ERIC) Clearing-house on Higher Education abstracts and indexes the current literature on higher education for inclusion in ERIC's database and announcement in ERIC's monthly bibliographic journal, *Resources in Education* (RIE). Most of these publications are available through the ERIC Document Reproduction Service (EDRS). For publications cited in this bibliography that are available from EDRS, ordering number and price code are included. Readers who wish to order a publication should write to the ERIC Document Reproduction Service, 7420 Fullerton Road, Suite 110, Springfield, Virginia 22153-2852. (Phone orders with VISA or MasterCard are taken at 800/443-ERIC or 703/440-1400.) When ordering, please specify the document (ED) number. Documents are available as noted in microfiche (MF) and paper copy (PC). If you have the price code ready when you call, EDRS can quote an exact price. The last page of the latest issue of *Resources in Education* also has the current cost, listed by code.

AAHE Assessment Forum. 1992. "Principles of Good Practice for Assessing Student Learning." Washington, D.C.: American Association for Higher Education.

Adamany, D. 1979. "Government Quality Programs and Effective Resource Use in Higher Education." Paper presented at the Annual Academic Planning Conference, June, University of Southern California, Los Angeles, California. ED 176 690. 38 pp. MF-01; PC-02.

Adelman, C.P., ed. 1985. *Assessment in American Higher Education: Issues and Contexts.* Washington, D.C.: U.S. Dept. of Education, Office of Educational Research and Improvement. ED 273 197. 90 pp. MF-01; PC-04.

————, ed. 1988. *Performance and Judgment: Essays on Principles and Practice in the Assessment of Student Learning.* Washington, D.C.: U.S. Dept. of Education, Office of Educational Research and Improvement. ED 299 888. 328 pp. MF-01; PC-14.

Alverno College Faculty. 1985. "Assessment at Alverno College." Milwaukee: Alverno Productions.

American Association of University Professors, Committee C. July/August 1991. "Mandated Assessment of Educational Outcomes: A Report of Committee C on College and University Teaching, Research, and Publication." *Academe* 4: 49–56.

Amiran, M., K.M. Schilling, and K.L. Schilling. 1993. "Assessing Outcomes of General Education." In *Making a Difference,* edited by T. Banta. San Francisco: Jossey-Bass.

Angelo, T.A. 1994. "Classroom Assessment: Involving Faculty and

Students Where It Matters Most." *Assessment Update* 6(4): 1–2+.

———. 1995. "Improving Classroom Assessment to Improve Learning: Guidelines from Research and Practice." *Assessment Update* 7(6): 1–2.

———. 1996. "Transforming Assessment: High Standards for Higher Learning." *AAHE Bulletin* 48(8): 3–4.

Angelo, T.A., and K.P. Cross. 1993. *Classroom Assessment Techniques: A Handbook for College Teachers.* 2d ed. San Francisco: Jossey-Bass.

Anrig, G.R. 1986. "A Message for Governors and State Legislators: The Minimum Competency Approach Can Be Bad for the Health of Higher Education." *AAHE Viewpoints.* ED 281 404. 9 pp. MF-01; PC-01.

———. 1993. "Access and Retention: Caring about Outcomes and Doing Something about Them." Paper presented at the AAHE National Conference on Higher Education, Washington, D.C.

Association of American Colleges. 1985. *Integrity in the College Curriculum: A Report to the Academic Community.* Washington, D.C.: Author. ED 251 059. 62 pp. MF-01; PC not available EDRS.

Astin, A.W. 1991. *Assessment for Excellence: The Philosophy and Practice of Assessment and Evaluation in Higher Education.* New York: ACE/Macmillan.

Bambenek, J.J. 1996. "Students as Assessors in Institutional Assessment." *Assessment Update* 8(3): 3.

Banta, T.W. 1985a. "Use of Outcomes Information at the University of Tennessee–Knoxville." In *Assessing Educational Outcomes,* edited by P.T. Ewell. New Directions for Institutional Research No. 47. San Francisco: Jossey-Bass.

———, ed. 1985b. *Performance Funding in Higher Education: A Case Study.* Boulder, Colo.: National Center for Higher Education Management Systems.

———, ed. 1986. *Performance Funding in Higher Education: A Critical Analysis of Tennessee's Experience.* Boulder, Colo.: National Center for Higher Education Management Systems. ED 310 655. 176 pp. MF-01; PC-08.

———, ed. 1988. *Implementing Outcomes Assessment: Promises and Perils.* New Directions for Institutional Research No. 59. San Francisco: Jossey-Bass.

———. 1989. "Weaving Assessment into the Fabric of Higher Education." *Assessment Update* 1(2): 3.

———. 1992. "Involving Faculty in Assessment." *Assessment Update* 5(1): 3–6.

———. 1995. "The Many Faces of Assessment Methodology." *As-*

sessment Update 7(2): 3+.

———. 1996. "Faculty Involvement in Assessment: Why Is It So Hard to Achieve?" *Assessment Update* 8(5): 3+.

Banta, T.W., and Associates, eds. 1993. *Making a Difference: Outcomes of a Decade of Assessment in Higher Education.* San Francisco: Jossey-Bass.

Banta, T.W., J.P. Lund, K.E. Black, and F.W. Oblander, eds. 1996. *Assessment in Practice: Putting Principles to Work on College Campuses.* San Francisco: Jossey-Bass.

Benjamin, E. 5 July 1990. "The Movement to Assess Students' Learning Will Institutionalize Mediocrity in Colleges." *Chronicle of Higher Education.*

Bok, D. 1986. *Higher Learning.* Cambridge, Mass.: Harvard Univ. Press.

Borden, V.M.H., and T.W. Banta. 1994. "Performance Indicators for Accountability and Improvement." In *Using Performance Indicators to Guide Strategic Decision Making,* edited by V.M.H. Borden and T.W. Banta. New Directions for Institutional Research No. 82. San Francisco: Jossey-Bass.

Boyer, C.M., et al. 1986. "Transforming the State Role in Improving Undergraduate Education: Time for a Different View." Denver: Education Commission of the States. ED 275 219. 45 pp. MF-01; PC not available EDRS.

Braskamp, L.A. 1991. "Purposes, Issues, and Principles of Assessment." *NCA Quarterly* 66(2): 417–29.

Burke, J. 1994. "Assessment: Vision's the Thing." In *Faculty Perspectives: Sharing Ideas on Assessment.* Albany: SUNY Faculty Senate.

Ciereszko, A.A. 1987. "Mandated Testing in Florida: A Faculty Perspective." In *Student Outcomes Assessment: What Institutions Stand to Gain,* edited by D.F. Halpern. New Directions for Higher Education No. 59. San Francisco: Jossey-Bass.

Cross, K.P. 1990. "Streams of Thought About Assessment." In *Assessment 1990: Understanding the Implications,* by K.P. Cross, G. Wiggins, and P. Hutchings. Washington, D.C.: AAHE Assessment Forum.

Cross, K.P., and T.A. Angelo. 1988. *Classroom Assessment Techniques: A Handbook for Faculty.* Ann Arbor: Univ. of Michigan, National Center for Research to Improve Postsecondary Teaching and Learning. ED 317 097. 166 pp. MF-01; PC-07.

Culver, S.M., and D.R. Ridley. 1995. "How to Guarantee the Failure of Assessment at Any Institution by Following 17 Easy, Proven Rules." *Assessment Update* 7(4): 3.

Eisenman, C. 1991. "Faculty Participation in Assessment Programs." *NCA Quarterly* 66(2): 458–64.

El-Khawas, E. 1992. *Campus Trends*. Higher Education Panel Report No. 82. Washington, D.C.: American Council on Education. ED 347 922. 93 pp. MF-01; PC-04.

Erwin, T.D. 1991. *Assessing Student Learning and Development: A Guide to the Principles, Goals, and Methods of Determining College Outcomes*. San Francisco: Jossey-Bass.

Ewell, P.T. 1983. *Information on Student Outcomes: How to Get It and How to Use It*. Boulder, Colo.: National Center for Higher Education Management Systems. ED 246 827. 89 pp. MF-01; PC-04.

———. 1984. *The Self-regarding Institution: Information for Excellence*. Boulder, Colo.: National Center for Higher Education Management Systems. ED 256 266. 110 pp. MF-01; PC-05.

———. 1985a. "Assessment: What's It All About?" *Change* 17(6): 32–36.

———, ed. 1985b. *Assessing Educational Outcomes*. New Directions for Institutional Research No. 47. San Francisco: Jossey-Bass.

———. 1987. "Assessment, Accountability, and Improvement: Managing the Contradiction." Paper presented at the Second National Conference on Assessment of the AAHE, Boulder, Colorado. ED 287 330. 25 pp. MF-01; PC-01.

———. 1991a. "Assessment and Public Accountability: Back to the Future." *Change* 23(6): 12–17.

———. 1991b. "To Capture the Ineffable: New Forms of Assessment in Higher Education." In *Reprise 1991: Reprints of Two Papers Treating Assessment's History and Implementation*. Washington, D.C.: American Association for Higher Education.

———. 1993a. "Performance Indicators: A New Round of Accountability." *Assessment Update* 5(3): 12.

———. 1993b. "The Role of States and Accreditors in Shaping Assessment Practice." In *Making a Difference: Outcomes of a Decade of Assessment in Higher Education*, edited by T.W. Banta and Associates. San Francisco: Jossey-Bass.

———. 1993c. "Total Quality and Academic Practice: The Idea We've Been Waiting For?" *Change* 25(3): 49–55.

———. 1996. "The Current Pattern of State-Level Assessment: Results of a National Inventory." *Assessment Update* 8(3): 1–2+.

———. 1997. "Assessment and Accountability in a Second Decade: New Looks or Same Old Stories?" Plenary address at the AAHE Assessment Forum, June, Miami Beach, Florida.

Ewell, P.T., and D. Jones. 1994. "Data, Indicators, and the National Center for Higher Education Management Systems." In *Using Performance Indicators to Guide Strategic Decision Making,* edited by V.H.M. Borden and T.W. Banta. New Directions for Institutional Research No. 82. San Francisco: Jossey-Bass.

Ewell, P.T., and R.P. Lisensky. 1988. *Assessing Institutional Effectiveness: Redirecting the Self-study Process.* Washington, D.C.: Consortium for the Advancement of Private Higher Education.

Feldman, K.A., and T.M. Newcomb. 1969. *The Impact of College on Students.* San Francisco: Jossey-Bass.

Ferren, A. 1993. "Faculty Resistance to Assessment: A Matter of Priorities and Perceptions." Conference discussion paper presented at the Double Feature Conference: 8th AAHE Conference on Assessment in Higher Education and 1st AAHE Continuous Quality Improvement Conference, June, Chicago, Illinois.

Gaff, J.G. 1991. *New Life for the College Curriculum: Assessing Achievements and Furthering Progress in the Reform of General Education.* San Francisco: Jossey-Bass.

Gaither, G., B.P. Nedwek, and J.E. Neal. 1994. *Measuring Up: The Promises and Pitfalls of Performance Indicators in Higher Education.* ASHE-ERIC Higher Education Report Volume 23, No. 5. Washington, D.C.: George Washington Univ., Graduate School of Education and Human Development. ED 383 279. 159 pp. MF-01; PC-07.

Gandolfo, Anita. 1995. "Formative Assessment: An Assessment Model That Answers the Questions." *Assessment Update* 7(2): 6–7.

Garcia, M. 1990. "Assessing Program Effectiveness in an Institution with a Diverse Student Body." In *The Effects of Assessment on Minority Student Participation,* edited by M.T. Nettles. New Directions for Institutional Research No. 65. San Francisco: Jossey-Bass.

Gardiner, L., C. Anderson, and B. Cambridge, eds. 1997. *Learning through Assessment: A Resource Guide for Higher Education.* Washington, D.C.: American Association for Higher Education.

Halpern, D.F., ed. 1987. *Student Outcomes Assessment: What Institutions Stand to Gain.* New Directions for Higher Education No. 59. San Francisco: Jossey-Bass.

Hexter, H., and P.J.K. Lippincott. 1990. "Campus and Student Assessment." *Research Briefs* 1: 1–18.

Hurtado, S., A. Astin, and E. Dey. 1991. "Varieties of General Education Programs: An Empirically Based Taxonomy." *Journal of General Education* 40: 133–62.

Hutchings, P. 1987. "Six Stories: Implementing Successful Assessment." Washington, D.C.: AAHE. ED 295 512. 21 pp. MF-01; PC-01.

———. July/August 1988. "Faculty Voices on Assessment." *Change:* 48–55.

———. 1989. "Behind Outcomes: Contexts and Questions for Assessment." Resource paper prepared for an AAHE Assessment Forum, June, Washington, D.C. ED 311 777. 31 pp. MF-01: PC-02.

———. 1990a. "Assessment and the Way We Work." In *Assessment 1990: Understanding the Implications,* by K.P. Cross, G. Wiggins, and P. Hutchings. Washington, D.C.: AAHE Assessment Forum.

———. 1990b. "Learning over Time: Portfolio Assessment." *AAHE Bulletin* 42(8): 6–8.

———. 1993. "Principles of Good Practice for Assessing Student Learning." *Assessment Update* 5(1): 6–7.

———. 1995. "From Results to Reflective Practice." *Assessment Update* 7(1): 1–3+.

Hutchings, P., and T. Marchese. 1990. "Watching Assessment: Questions, Stories, Prospects." *Change* 22(4): 12–38.

Hutchings, P., T. Marchese, and B. Wright. 1991. "Using Assessment to Strengthen General Education." AAHE Assessment Forum. Washington, D.C.: American Association for Higher Education.

Hutchings, P., and E. Reuben. July/August 1988. "Faculty Voices in Assessment." *Change.*

Jacobi, M.A., A. Astin, and F. Ayala, Jr. 1987. *College Student Outcomes Assessment: A Talent Development Perspective.* ASHE-ERIC Higher Education Report No. 7. Washington, D.C.: Association for the Study of Higher Education. ED 296 693. 141 pp. MF-01: PC-06.

Jencks, C., and D. Riesman. 1968. *The Academic Revolution.* Garden City, N.Y.: Doubleday.

Johnson, R., J. Prus, R. Andersen, and E. El-Khawas. 1991. "Assessing Assessment: An In-depth Status Report on the Higher Education Assessment Movement." Washington, D.C.: American Council on Education. ED 332 625. 36 pp. MF-01; PC-02.

Jones, E.A., S. Hoffman, L.M. Moore, G. Ratcliff, S. Tibbetts, and B.A. Click. 1994. *Essential Skills in Writing, Speech and Listening, and Critical Thinking for College Graduates: Perspectives of Faculty, Employers, and Policymakers.* Contract No. R117G10037. Washington, D.C.: U.S. Dept. of Education, Office of Educational Research and Improvement. ED 383 255. 193 pp. MF-01; PC-08.

Knefelkamp, L.L., P.T. Ewell, and R. Brown. 1989. "Three Presentations from the Fourth National Conference on Assessment in Higher Education." Washington, D.C.: AAHE Assessment Forum.

Levy, R.A. 1986. "Development of Performance Funding Criteria." In *Performance Funding in Higher Education: A Critical Analysis of Tennessee's Experience,* edited by T.W. Banta. Boulder, Colo.: National Center for Higher Education Management Systems.

Light, R.J. 1990. "The Harvard Assessment Seminars: Explorations with Students and Faculty about Teaching, Learning, and Student Life." First report. Cambridge, Mass.: Harvard Univ. Graduate School of Education/Kennedy School of Government.

―――. 1992. "Harvard Assessment Seminars: Explorations with Students and Faculty about Teaching, Learning, and Student Life." Second report. Cambridge, Mass.: Harvard Univ. Graduate School of Education.

Loacker, G. 1988. "Faculty as a Force to Improve Instruction through Assessment." In *Assessing Students' Learning,* edited by J.H. McMillan. New Directions for Teaching and Learning No. 34. San Francisco: Jossey-Bass.

Loacker, G., and M. Mentkowski. 1993. "Creating a Culture Where Assessment Improves Learning." In *Making a Difference,* edited by T.W. Banta. San Francisco: Jossey-Bass.

Lynton, E.A. 1994. "The Changing Nature of Universities." *New England Journal of Public Policy* 10(1): 241–50.

McMillan, J.H., ed. 1988. *Assessing Students' Learning.* New Directions for Teaching and Learning No. 34. San Francisco: Jossey-Bass.

Marchese, T. 1987. "Third Down, Ten Years to Go." *AAHE Bulletin* 40(4): 3–8.

―――. October 1988. "Perspectives on General Education and Its Assessment." *AAHE Bulletin* 41(2): 6–9.

―――. May 1994. "What Is the Status of Assessment Today?" Keynote address. In *Faculty Perspectives: Sharing Ideas on Assessment.* Albany: SUNY Faculty Senate.

Marcus, D. 1990. *Lessons Learned from FIPSE Projects.* Washington, D.C.: U.S. Dept. of Education, Fund for the Improvement of Postsecondary Education.

Marcus, D., E.B. Cobb, and R.E. Shoenberg. 1993, 1996. *Lessons Learned from FIPSE Projects II and III.* Washington, D.C.: U.S. Dept. of Education, Fund for the Improvement of Postsecondary Education. ED 403 841. 181 pp. MF-01; PC-08.

Mentkowski, M., and G. Loacker. 1985. "Assessing and Validating the Outcomes of College." In *Assessing Educational Outcomes,* edited by P. Ewell. New Directions for Institutional Research No. 47. San Francisco: Jossey-Bass.

Merriam, S.B. 1988. *Case Study Research in Education: A Qualitative Approach*. San Francisco: Jossey-Bass.

Miller, R.I. 1988. "Using Change Strategies to Implement Assessment Programs." In *Implementing Outcomes Assessment: Promise and Perils*, edited by T.W. Banta. New Directions for Educational Research No. 9. San Francisco: Jossey-Bass.

Muffo, J.A. 1991. "The Status of Student Outcomes Assessment at NASULGC Member Institutions." Presentation at the Annual Forum of the Association for Institutional Research, May, San Francisco, California. ED 336 032. 23 pp. MF-01; PC-01.

———. 1996. "Lessons Learned from a Decade of Assessment." *Assessment Update* 8(5): 1–2+. ED 397 716. 18 pp. MF-01; PC-01.

Musil, C.M., ed. 1992. *Students at the Center: Feminist Assessment*. Washington, D.C.: Association of American Colleges. ED 353 883. 126 pp. MF-01; PC not available EDRS.

National Governors Association. 1986. *Time for Results: The Governors' 1991 Report on Education*. Washington, D.C.: Author.

Nettles, M.T., ed. 1990. *The Effects of Assessment on Minority Student Participation*. New Directions for Institutional Research No. 65. San Francisco: Jossey-Bass.

Nettles, M.T., and A.L. Nettles, eds. 1995. *Equity and Excellence in Educational Testing and Assessment*. Norwell, Mass.: Kluwer Academic Publishers.

Nichols, J.O. 1991. *The Departmental Guide to Implementation of Student Outcomes Assessment and Institutional Effectiveness*. New York: Agathon Press.

North Central Regional Educational Lab. May 1996. "The Status of State Student Assessment Programs in the United States." Annual report. State Student Assessment Program Database for School Year 1994–95. TM026132. Oak Brook, Ill.: Author.

Nowaczyk, R.H., and J.D. Frey. 1982. "Factors Related to Performance on the GRE Advanced Psychology Test." *Teaching of Psychology* 9: 163–65.

Pace, C.R. 1979. *Measuring Outcomes of College: Fifty Years of Findings and Recommendations for the Future*. San Francisco: Jossey-Bass.

Palomba, C., and D. Moore. 1996. "Summer Assessment Grant Program for Faculty." In *Assessment in Practice: Putting Principles to Work on College Campuses*, edited by T.W. Banta, J.P. Lund, K.E. Black, and F.W. Oblander. San Francisco: Jossey-Bass.

Pascarella, E.T., and P.T. Terenzini. 1991. *How College Affects Students: Findings and Insights from Twenty Years of Research*. San Francisco: Jossey-Bass.

Paskow, J., ed. 1988. *Assessment Programs and Projects: A Directory.* Washington, D.C.: American Association for Higher Education.

Peters, Roger. 1994. "Some Snarks Are Boojums: Accountability and the End(s) of Higher Education." *Change* 26(6): 16–23.

Project on Strong Foundations for General Education. 1994. *Strong Foundations: Twelve Principles for Effective General Education Programs.* Washington, D. C.: Association of American Colleges. ED 367 250. 90 pp. MF-01; PC not available EDRS.

Ratcliff, J.L., E.A. Jones, and S. Hoffman. 1992. *Handbook on Linking Assessment and General Education.* University Park, Pa.: National Center on Postsecondary Teaching, Learning, and Assessment. ED 357 700. 122 pp. MF-01; PC-05.

Resnick, D., and M. Goulden. 1987. "Assessment, Curriculum, and Expansion in American Higher Education: A Historical Perspective." In *Student Outcomes Assessment: What Institutions Stand to Gain,* edited by D. Halpern. New Directions for Higher Education No. 59. San Francisco: Jossey-Bass.

Rice, R.E. 1996. *Making a Place for the New American Scholar.* Washington, D.C.; American Association for Higher Education.

Robertson, S.N., and C.A. Simpson. 1996. "General Education Discipline Evaluation Process for the Community College." In *Assessment in Practice: Putting Principles to Work on College Campuses,* edited by T.W. Banta, J.P. Lund, K.E. Black, and F.W. Oblander. San Francisco: Jossey-Bass.

Rogers, G. 1994. "Measurement and Judgement in Curricular Assessment Systems." *Assessment Update* 6(1): 6–7.

Rudolph, F. 1984. "The Power of Professors: The Impact of Specialization and Professionalization on the Curriculum." *Change* 16(4): 12–17.

Schilling, K.M., and K.L. Schilling. 1993a. "Descriptive Approaches to Assessment: Moving beyond Meeting Requirements to Making a Difference." In *A Collection of Papers on Self-study and Institutional Improvements.* Chicago: North Central Association of Colleges and Schools. ED 356 712. 214 pp. MF-01; PC-09.

———. 24 March 1993b. "Professors Must Respond to Calls for Accountability." *Chronicle of Higher Education:* A40.

———. 1997. "Looking Back/Moving Ahead: Assessment in the Senior Year." In *The Senior Year: A Beginning, Not an End,* edited by J. Gardner and G. Van der Veer. San Francisco: Jossey-Bass.

Seybert, J.A., and D.F. Soltz. 1996. "Assessment of Developmental Programs." In *Assessment in Practice: Putting Principles to Work on College Campuses,* edited by T.W. Banta, J.P. Lund, K.E. Black, and F.W. Oblander. San Francisco: Jossey-Bass.

Shapiro, J.P. 1992. "What Is Feminist Assessment?" In *Students at the Center: Feminist Assessment,* edited by C.M. Musil. Washington D.C. Association of American Colleges.

Shulman, L.S., V.B. Smith, and D.M. Stewart. 1987. "Three Presentations from the Second National Conference on Assessment in Higher Education." Washington, D.C.: AAHE Assessment Forum.

Smith, D.G. 1990. "The Challenge of Diversity: Implications for Institutional Research." In *The Effects of Assessment on Minority Student Participation,* edited by M.T. Nettles. New Directions for Institutional Research No. 65. San Francisco: Jossey-Bass.

Smith, E.D. 1996. "What Makes a Good Assessment Program?" *Assessment Update* 8(1): 4–5.

Spear, K., A. Ferren, and J. Romano. 1992. "After the Romance: Starting and Sustaining Liberal Education Reform." *Perspectives* 22(1): 89–103.

Stark, J.S., K.M. Shaw, and M.A. Lowther. 1989. *Student Goals for College and Courses: A Missing link in Assessing and Improving Academic Achievement.* ASHE-ERIC Higher Education Report No. 6. Washington, D.C.: George Washington Univ., Graduate School of Education and Human Resources. ED 317 121. 132 pp. MF-01; PC-06.

Stark, J.S., and A. Thomas. 1994. *Assessment and Program Evaluation.* ASHE Reader Series. Needham Heights, Mass.: Simon & Schuster Custom Publishing.

Steele, J.M. 1996. "Postsecondary Assessment Needs: Implications for State Policy." *Assessment Update* 8(2): 1–2+.

Stevens, G., and T.J. Haas. 1996. "Assessing the Institution: The Federal Service Academy Model." *Assessment Update* 8(2): 4–5.

Study Group on the Conditions of Excellence in American Higher Education. 1984. *Involvement in Learning: Realizing the Potential of American Higher Education.* Washington, D.C.: U.S. Dept. of Education, National Institute of Education. ED 246 833. 127 pp. MF-01; PC-06.

Tafel, J., and K.L. Schilling. 1992. "Assessing the Characteristics of High-Quality Programs: Lessons from the Ohio Board of Regents FIPSE Study." *Assessment Update* 4(6): 14.

Tarule, J.T., and M.K.T. Tetreault. 1992. "Assessment Designs and the Courage to Innovate." In *Students at the Center: Feminist Assessment,* edited by C.M. Musil. Washington, D.C.: Association of American Colleges.

Tierney, W.G. 1989. "Cultural Politics and the Curriculum in Postsecondary Education." *Journal of Education* 171(3): 72–88.

———, ed. 1998. *The Responsive University: Restructuring for High*

Performance. Baltimore: Johns Hopkins Univ. Press.

Wergin, J. 1989. "Politics of Assessment in the University." *Assessment Update* 1(2): 5–7.

Wiggins, G. 1989. "A True Test: Toward More Authentic and Equitable Assessment." *Phi Delta Kappan* 70: 703–13.

———. 1990. "The Truth May Make You Free, but the Test May Keep You Imprisoned." In *Assessment 1990: Understanding the Implications,* by K.P. Cross, G. Wiggins, and P. Hutchings. Washington, D.C.: AAHE Assessment Forum.

———. 1993. *Assessing Student Performance: Exploring the Purpose and Limits of Testing*. San Francisco: Jossey-Bass.

Wolff, R.A., and A.W. Astin. 1990. *Assessment 1990: Accreditation and Renewal*. Washington, D.C.: AAHE Assessment Forum.

Wolff, R.A., and O.D. Harris. 1994. "Using Assessment to Develop a Culture of Evidence." In *Changing College Classrooms: New Teaching and Learning Strategies for an Increasingly Complex World,* edited by D.F. Halpern et al. San Francisco: Jossey-Bass.

Young, C.C., and M.E. Knight. 1993. "Providing Leadership for Organizational Change." In *Making a Difference,* edited by T. Banta. San Francisco: Jossey-Bass.

Zguta, R. 1989. "Faculty Response to Assessment at a Major Research University." *Assessment Update* 1(3): 7–9.

INDEX

A

AAUP's Committee C statement on mandated assessment, 46, 64

Academic Profile, 47, 49

accountability, changing notions of, 59–60

ACT-COMP, 47

>mandated testing with, 8

>use at Miami University, 49

ACT survey of assessment programs

>results disappointing, 17

administrative leadership consequences, 71–72

afraid of change as factor in faculty resistance to assessment, 18

Alverno College, 33

>assessment as part of an institution's fabric at, 72–73

>assessment a transforming lever at, 62–63

>curriculum based on performance for identified abilities, 5

>development of outcomes measures for campus programs, 53

>very successful emphasis on assessment as learning, 13

American college students most tested in the world, 1

American higher education had two major assessment movements, 5

Anrig, Gregory, 27

appropriate language and metaphors, 89–90

assessment

>and Quality Improvement, link between, 38–39

>and teaching practice, tie between, 35–38

>approaches that lead to improvement of higher education, 29

>centers focused on assessment of human performance, 5

>coordinating networks function, 12

>core focus on improving teaching and learning, 2

>forum of the AAHE brought focus to key issues, 11–12

>growth in requirements for, 15–16

>inconsistent with values factor in faculty resistance, 19–20

>movement positive result, 14

>practice frameworks, eight major shifts in, 25

>process underlying assumptions determine its results, x

>range of meanings, 1–2

>rationale for faculty reluctance to become involved in, 16

>requires understanding of knowing within discipline, 32

>six traditions, 5

>success more likely when a means rather than an end, 69

>two traditions of, 59

>violates academic freedom as factor in faculty resistance, 19

Continuous Quality Improvement, 38

"corporatist" model of higher education, 59–60

credible evidence and forms of judgment, 88–89

criteria unclear factor in faculty resistance to assessment, 18–19

Cross, K. Patricia, 35–36

cultural transformation, assessment as a tool in, 43

cumulative and incremental models of understanding
        need to commit to, 92

curriculum objectives, importance of testing for, 49

D

data misuse as factor in faculty resistance to assessment, 18

distributional models of general education far more common than
  core curricular models, 47

don't need more bureaucracy factor in faculty resistance to
  assessment, 21

Doonesbury, issues relating to faculty workload and lack of
  attention to student treated in, 15

E

ECS. *See* Education Commission of the States.

Education Commission of the States, 7

Educational Testing Service, 27

Ewell (1993b) description of reaction to new higher education
  assessment mandates, 8–9

excellence as a function of how well educate students, 26

excellence in higher education
        three critical conditions, 6

Exxon Foundation supported important assessment initiatives, 13

F

faculty
        aversion to assessment, rationale for, ix
        identification of assessment as an integral part of their role
          six conditions necessary for, 85
        involvement key to success in assessment, 93
        lack knowledge of assessment factor in faculty resistance, 20
        ownership of data one of the most important factors in
          the success of assessment, 54, 64
        role in assessment, 2–4

false starts incurring hostility, 63–68

feminist assessment, effects of assessment on, 41–43

FIPSE. *See* Fund for the Improvement of Post-Secondary Education.

J

James Madison University Office of Assessment, 78

Jencks and Riesman model, 14

Johnson City Community College Office of Institutional Research, 78–79

Johnson, Reid
provided leadership to help establish national
prominence of South Carolina network, 12

K

Kean College of New Jersey
assessment as part of an institution's fabric at, 73
development of local measures of outcomes, 53

Kellogg Foundation supported important assessment initiatives, 13

King's College of New Jersey
assessment as part of an institution's fabric at, 73
assessment has been a transforming lever at, 62–63

L

leadership at Northeast Missouri State University, 73–74

Lessons Learned from FIPSE Projects, 13

Light (1990) successful in identifying assessment with naturally
occurring conversations about teaching and learning, 89

local culture, assessment practices tied to, 93

Lowell, A. Lawrence president of Harvard, 4

M

major components of traditional faculty role, 3

manageable chunks, good assessment proceeds by identifying, 92

mandated assessment, statement on, 46, 64

Marchese, Ted, 38

meaningful assessment raises as many questions as it answers, 92

measurement and judgment, clear distinction between, 56–57

measurement theory and practice
overview of many prominent large-scale studies, 5

Miami University, 13, 49
assessment program began with questions about effectiveness of two common models of general education, 79–80

minimal competency testing
failure of, 27–29
four reasons why would not work for higher education,
28–29

minority students, effects of assessment on, 40–41

Missouri documents improvements from state-mandated assessment, 10
models of incentive funding, 13
most tested in the world, American college students are the, 1
multiple measures advantage, 52
multiple measures of performance, 50–52
multiple perspectives as valid approaches to assessment recognize and accommodate, 93

N

NASULGC. *See* National Association of State Universities and Land-Grant Colleges.
National Association of State Universities and Land-Grant Colleges
    best known assessment programs at small colleges and less selective universities, 13–14
    identified several problems with assessment, 16–17
National Center for Higher Education Management Systems, 8
National Governors Association support for broadly based standardized testing, 7
nature of faculty, accommodating assessment to, 90–91
Nettles on effects of assessment on minority students, 40
nobody told me about the shift from teachers and teaching to students and learning as factor in faculty resistance to assessment, 21–22
no confidence in existing instruments as factor in faculty resistance to assessment, 20–21
Northeast Missouri State University
    assessment as part of an institution's fabric at, 73–74
    assessment has been a transforming lever at, 62–63
Northern Virginia Community College
    development of general education assessment at, 81–82
Northwest Missouri State University
    Total Quality Management at, 38

O

Ohio State Program Excellence competitions, 77
ongoing process, need to commit to, 92
optimal use of existing data before collecting new data, 92

P

Pace (1979) overview of many prominent large-scale studies in measurement theory and practice, 5

peer review
      as a way to engage in quality control, 6
      as the preferred approach to evaluating effectiveness, 56
performance indicator, 61
      driving models of funding for higher education in 25
         states, 61
      faculty resistance to, 61
      move to, 60–62
plate is too full as factor in faculty resistance to assessment, 21
power and policies surrounding decisions, 40
pressures to credit prior experience and to facilitate articulation and
   transfer as challenges faculty face, 87–88
"Principles of Good Practice for Assessing Student Learning," 12
private benefit, higher education as, 60
problem in separating process and content in trying to understand
   learning, 31
program monitoring involving large-scale longitudinal studies, 5
public utility, higher education as a, 59

Q

questioning how the competence of graduates could be assured
   with the demise of the senior declamation, 4
questions of interest to the faculty, 86–88

R

rational choice model, 29
reflective practice, assessment as a stimulus to, 90
Reid, Sister Joel
      leadership at Alverno College, 72–73
"Report on Mandated Assessment," 53–54
"resource" or "reputational" views, 25
rising junior exam (College Level Academic Skills Test), 75–76
role for faculty, principles for envisioning assessment as, 91–93

S

scholarship of application, Boyer's notion of, 79
scholarship of representation, 67
scholarship on development of understanding in a discipline
   must be done by practitioners of discipline, 32
scores on standardized measures of general education don't
   measure curriculum's effectiveness, 48
self-examination best conducted in a climate free of external
   constraint or threats, 64

senior declamation, demise of, 4–5

"senior examiner," 5

service as least valued of the components of the faculty role, 3

Shulman, Lee, 31

sources of faculty resistance to assessment programs, 17–22

South Carolina

> establishment of assessment coordinating networks by, 12
>
> will potentially use 37 performance indicators to determine allocation of resources to public higher education, 61

South Dakota Board of Regents mandated testing with ACT-COMP at end of sophomore year, 8

standardized measurement instruments that are easiest to replicate are least valid except for assessment of basic skills, 46

standardized testing, 5

Stanford University, 31

state mandates

> may be credited with providing major impetus to development of assessment practices in higher education, 10

Statement on Assessment by AAUP, 1

student achievement

> U.S. Dept. of Education insistence that regional and programmatic accrediting bodies require information on, 10–11

student and learning processes, focus on, 33–35

student development over the college years, studies, 5

student learning

> as opposed to incoming selectivity as model for academic institution determination, 14
>
> standards commitment absence as an impediment to institutionalizing assessment, 63

student outcomes

> higher education community saw little point but no small threat in explicit assessment of, 16

Students at the Center, 41

success of assessment

> faculty ownership of data as most important factor in, 54

SUNY–Freedonia, assessment at, 80

supportive fiscal and policy context for assessment, 85–86

sure route to nowhere when assessment is add-on activity unrelated to regular work of faculty and students, 34

Swarthmore "senior examiner," 5

T

talent development. *See* value-added perspective.

talent development model of assessment
  what most faculty see as their role and responsibilities, 27
teaching to the test, focus on test scores invokes response of, 48
Tennessee
  able to document program improvements resulting from
    state-mandated assessment, 10
  goal-oriented performance funding model for its state
    university system, 60–61
testing in a local context, 45–50
Tierney (1998) important role for assessment in a changed culture
  in academy, 43
Time for Results, 8
Total Quality Management, 38
traditional faculty role, major components of, 3
*Transforming the State Role in Improving Undergraduate Edu-
  cation*, 7
"triangulation," 51
Trudeau, Garry, 15
Trudy Banta led response to performance funding at University
  of Tennessee–Knoxville, 76
Truman State University. *See* Northeast Missouri State University.

U

unexamined college or university not worth attending, 93
unfunded mandate, assessment as, 67
Union College, assessment as opportunity for teaching at, 82
University of California at Berkeley, 36
University of Connecticut, 13
University of Maryland
  Office of Assessment functioning at, 78
  Total Quality Management at, 38
University of Tennessee
  local measures of outcomes for various campus programs,
    53
University of Tennessee–Knoxville
  Trudy Banta led response to performance funding at, 76

V

value-added perspective, 25–27
Virginia
  establishment of assessment coordinating networks by, 12
  highly decentralized approach to quality improvement, 9
Virginia Military Institute Office of Assessment, 78

vision absence as impediment to institutionalizing assessment, 63

ASHE-ERIC HIGHER EDUCATION REPORTS

Since 1983, the Association for the Study of Higher Education (ASHE) and the Educational Resources Information Center (ERIC) Clearinghouse on Higher Education, a sponsored project of the Graduate School of Education and Human Development at The George Washington University, have cosponsored the ASHE-ERIC Higher Education Report series. This volume is the twenty-sixth overall and the ninth to be published by the Graduate School of Education and Human Development at The George Washington University.

Each monograph is the definitive analysis of a tough higher education problem, based on thorough research of pertinent literature and institutional experiences. Topics are identified by a national survey. Noted practitioners and scholars are then commissioned to write the reports, with experts providing critical reviews of each manuscript before publication.

Eight monographs (10 before 1985) in the ASHE-ERIC Higher Education Report series are published each year and are available on individual and subscription bases. To order, use the order form on the last page of this book.

Qualified persons interested in writing a monograph for the ASHE-ERIC Higher Education Report series are invited to submit a proposal to the National Advisory Board. As the preeminent literature review and issue analysis series in higher education, the Higher Education Reports are guaranteed wide dissemination and national exposure for accepted candidates. Execution of a monograph requires at least a minimal familiarity with the ERIC database, including *Resources in Education* and the current *Index to Journals in Education*. The objective of these reports is to bridge conventional wisdom with practical research. Prospective authors are strongly encouraged to call Dr. Fife at (800) 773-3742.

For further information, write to
   ASHE-ERIC Higher Education Report Series
   The George Washington University
   One Dupont Circle, Suite 630
   Washington, DC 20036-1183
Or phone (202) 296-2597 ext. 13;
toll free: (800) 773-ERIC ext. 13.

Write or call for a complete catalog.

Visit our Web site at **www.gwu.edu/~eriche/Reports**

ADVISORY BOARD

James Earl Davis
University of Delaware at Newark

Kenneth A. Feldman
State University of New York–Stony Brook

Kassie Freeman
Peabody College, Vanderbilt University

Susan Frost
Emory University

Kenneth P. Gonzalez
Arizona State University

Esther E. Gotlieb
West Virginia University

Philo Hutcheson
Georgia State University

J. Roderick Lauver
Planned Systems International, Inc.

Clara M. Lovett
Northern Arizona University

Laurence R. Marcus
Rowan College

Robert Menges
Northwestern University

Diane E. Morrison
Centre for Curriculum, Transfer, and Technology

John A. Muffo
Virginia Tech

L. Jackson Newell
University of Utah

Steven G. Olswang
University of Washington

Laura W. Perna
Frederick D. Patterson Research
  Institute of the College Fund/UNCF

R. Eugene Rice
American Association for Higher Education

Sherry Sayles-Folks
Eastern Michigan University

Jack H. Schuster
Claremont Graduate School–Center for Educational Studies

Marilla D. Svinicki
University of Texas–Austin

David Sweet
OERI, U.S. Department of Education

Jon E. Travis
Texas A&M University

Dan W. Wheeler
University of Nebraska–Lincoln

Donald H. Wulff
University of Washington

Manta Yorke
Liverpool John Moores University

REVIEW PANEL

Richard Alfred
University of Michigan

Robert J. Barak
Iowa State Board of Regents

Alan Bayer
Virginia Polytechnic Institute and State University

John P. Bean
Indiana University–Bloomington

John M. Braxton
Peabody College, Vanderbilt University

Ellen M. Brier
Tennessee State University

Dennis Brown
University of Kansas

Patricia Carter
University of Michigan

John A. Centra
Syracuse University

Paul B. Chewning
Council for the Advancement and Support of Education

Arthur W. Chickering
Vermont College

Darrel A. Clowes
Virginia Polytechnic Institute and State University

Deborah M. DiCroce
Piedmont Virginia Community College

Dorothy E. Finnegan
The College of William & Mary

Kenneth C. Green
Claremont Graduate University

James C. Hearn
University of Georgia

Edward R. Hines
Illinois State University

Deborah Hunter
University of Vermont

Linda K. Johnsrud
University of Hawaii at Manoa

Bruce Anthony Jones
University of Missouri–Columbia

Elizabeth A. Jones
West Virginia University

Marsha V. Krotseng
State College and University Systems of West Virginia

George D. Kuh
Indiana University–Bloomington

J. Roderick Lauver
Planned Systems International, Inc.–Maryland

Daniel T. Layzell
MGT of America, Inc., Madison, Wisconsin

Patrick G. Love
Kent State University

Meredith Jane Ludwig
Education Statistics Services Institute

Mantha V. Mehallis
Florida Atlantic University

Toby Milton
Essex Community College

John A. Muffo
Virginia Polytechnic Institute and State University

L. Jackson Newell
Deep Springs College

Mark Oromaner
Hudson Community College

James C. Palmer
Illinois State University

Robert A. Rhoads
Michigan State University

G. Jeremiah Ryan
Quincy College

Mary Ann Danowitz Sagaria
The Ohio State University

Kathryn Nemeth Tuttle
University of Kansas

RECENT TITLES

Volume 26 ASHE-ERIC Higher Education Reports

1. Faculty Workload Studies: Perspectives, Needs, and Future Directions
   Katrina A. Meyer

2. Assessing Faculty Publication Productivity: Issues of Equity
   Elizabeth G. Creamer

Volume 25 ASHE-ERIC Higher Education Reports

1. A Culture for Academic Excellence: Implementing the Quality Principles in Higher Education
   Jann E. Freed, Marie R. Klugman, and Jonathan D. Fife

2. From Discipline to Development: Rethinking Student Conduct in Higher Education
   Michael Dannells

3. Academic Controversy: Enriching College Instruction through Intellectual Conflict
   David W. Johnson, Roger T. Johnson, and Karl A. Smith

4. Higher Education Leadership: Analyzing the Gender Gap
   Luba Chliwniak

5. The Virtual Campus: Technology and Reform in Higher Education
   Gerald C. Van Dusen

6. Early Intervention Programs: Opening the Door to Higher Education
   Robert H. Fenske, Christine A. Geranios, Jonathan E. Keller, and David E. Moore

7. The Vitality of Senior Faculty Members: Snow on the Roof—Fire in the Furnace
   Carole J. Bland and William H. Bergquist

8. A National Review of Scholastic Achievement in General Education: How Are We Doing and Why Should We Care?
   Steven J. Osterlind

Volume 24 ASHE-ERIC Higher Education Reports

1. Tenure, Promotion, and Reappointment: Legal and Administrative Implications
   Benjamin Baez and John A. Centra

2. Taking Teaching Seriously: Meeting the Challenge of Instructional Improvement
   Michael B. Paulsen and Kenneth A. Feldman

3. Empowering the Faculty: Mentoring Redirected and Renewed
   Gaye Luna and Deborah L. Cullen

4. Enhancing Student Learning: Intellectual, Social, and Emotional Integration
   Anne Goodsell Love and Patrick G. Love

5. Benchmarking in Higher Education: Adapting Best Practices to Improve Quality
   Jeffrey W. Alstete

6. Models for Improving College Teaching: A Faculty Resource
   Jon E. Travis

7. Experiential Learning in Higher Education: Linking Classroom and Community
   Jeffrey A. Cantor

8. Successful Faculty Development and Evaluation: The Complete Teaching Portfolio
   John P. Murray

Volume 23 ASHE-ERIC Higher Education Reports

1. The Advisory Committee Advantage: Creating an Effective Strategy for Programmatic Improvement
   Lee Teitel

2. Collaborative Peer Review: The Role of Faculty in Improving College Teaching
   Larry Keig and Michael D. Waggoner

3. Prices, Productivity, and Investment: Assessing Financial Strategies in Higher Education
   Edward P. St. John

4. The Development Officer in Higher Education: Toward an Understanding of the Role
   Michael J. Worth and James W. Asp II

5. Measuring Up: The Promises and Pitfalls of Performance Indicators in Higher Education
   Gerald Gaither, Brian P. Nedwek, and John E. Neal

6. A New Alliance: Continuous Quality and Classroom Effectiveness
   Mimi Wolverton

7. Redesigning Higher Education: Producing Dramatic Gains in Student Learning
   Lion F. Gardiner

8. Student Learning outside the Classroom: Transcending Artificial Boundaries
   George D. Kuh, Katie Branch Douglas, Jon P. Lund, and Jackie Ramin-Gyurnek

Volume 22 ASHE-ERIC Higher Education Reports

1. The Department Chair: New Roles, Responsibilities, and Challenges
   Alan T. Seagren, John W. Creswell, and Daniel W. Wheeler

Quantity   **Amount**

_____ Please begin my subscription to the current year's *ASHE-ERIC Higher Education Reports* at $120.00, over 33% off the cover price, starting with Report 1. _____

_____ Please send a complete set of Volume ___ *ASHE-ERIC Higher Education Reports* at $120.00, over 33% off the cover price. _____

Individual reports are available for $24.00 and include the cost of shipping and handling.

SHIPPING POLICY:

- Books are sent UPS Ground or equivalent. For faster delivery, call for charges.
- Alaska, Hawaii, U.S. Territories, and Foreign Countries, please call for shipping information.
- Order will be shipped within 24 hours after receipt of request.
- Orders of 10 or more books, call for shipping information.

All prices shown are subject to change.

Returns: No cash refunds—credit will be applied to future orders.

PLEASE SEND ME THE FOLLOWING REPORTS:

Quantity	Volume/No.	Title	Amount

Please check one of the following:

☐ Check enclosed, payable to GW-ERIC.   **Subtotal:** _____

☐ Purchase order attached.   **Less Discount:** _____

☐ Charge my credit card indicated below: **Total Due:** _____

   ☐ Visa   ☐ MasterCard

☐☐☐☐☐☐☐☐☐☐☐☐☐☐☐☐

Expiration Date_____

Name_____

Title_____

Institution_____

Address_____

City _____ State _____ Zip_____

Phone _____ Fax _____Telex_____

Signature _____ Date_____

SEND ALL ORDERS TO: ASHE-ERIC Higher Education Reports Series
The George Washington University
One Dupont Cir., Ste. 630, Washington, DC 20036-1183
Phone: (202) 296-2597 ext. 13
Toll-free: (800) 773-ERIC ext. 13
FAX: (202) 452-1844
URL: www.gwu.edu/~eriche/Reports